ESTATE PLANNING FOR THE MODERN FAMILY

A Georgian's Guide to Wills, Trusts, and Powers of Attorney

John P. Farrell, Esq.

This book is a work of fiction. Names, characters, places, and incidents either are products of the author's imagination or are used fictitiously. Any resemblance to actual persons, living or dead, events, or locales is entirely coincidental.

John P. Farrell, Esq.
Visit my website at www.TheFarrellLawFirm.com/home/

Printed in the United States of America

First Printing: July 2018
The Farrell Law Firm, P.C.

ISBN: 978-1-71774-915-4

INTRODUCTION

Imagine the patriarch of the family is in his second marriage. He is retired from a business he currently owns and has several children. Imagine two of his children are grown, married, and from his first marriage. One of his children is a toddler and is from his second marriage. Also, imagine he is the stepfather to a child born to his second wife.

Now, imagine his daughter runs the business he created and owns. She is married to a man who is a real estate agent and they have three children together.

His son is in a same-sex marriage and he and his partner have adopted a daughter.

Imagine from one man you have a second marriage, retiree, raising a toddler, stepson, married daughter, same-sex marriage, adoption, and grandchildren. Sounds like the makings of a good sitcom, doesn't it?

Today's families are much more complex than in times past. While your family may not include each of the above circumstance, there's a fair chance your family contains one or more of them. For this reason, estate planning cannot be cookie-cutter and each estate plan needs to be individualized for your particular family, the modern family.

This book is dedicated to my family. Most importantly, to my wife, Stacey, and my two boys, Jack and Liam.

Stacey, a lawyer herself, has been instrumental in my success. Having an opportunity to share a law practice with her is a true blessing. Without a doubt, she is a better lawyer than I am and has been gracious with her time and knowledge when I wanted to discuss ideas about this book with her. As a general rule, you should always surround yourself with people who are better than you and Stacey is willing to tolerate me in this regard.

To Jack and Liam, who inspire me in many ways, I am extremely grateful. The word 'legacy' comes up a lot with estate planning. I couldn't be more proud of Jack and Liam who are so special in their own way. There's truly nothing more I enjoy than sitting around the dinner table with my family and hearing about their day. I hope they will be interested in doing that for many more years.

To my dad, mom, brother, and sister, I give many thanks for having put up with my eccentric ways.

exegi monumentum aere perennius
regalique situ pyramidum altius,
quod non imber edax, non Aquilo inpotens
possit diruere...
(Odes III: XXX, lines 1-4, published 23BC)

DISCLAIMER

This book is not intended to be legal advice. The information contained within this book is for educational purposes only. Before making any legal decisions, you should first consult a qualified estate planning attorney.

ABOUT THE AUTHOR

John P. Farrell is an Estate Planning Attorney with Farrell Law where he serves clients in the Metro Atlanta area through the firm's Marietta, Georgia office. John is a native Georgian and currently lives in Marietta with his wife and two sons. He was born and raised in Calhoun, Georgia and moved to the Atlanta area twenty-five years ago to attend Kennesaw State University where he received his Bachelor's Degree in Political Science. He received his law degree from Georgia State University College of Law in Atlanta. John has practiced law since 2003 and is licensed in Georgia, Tennessee, and Texas. Over the years, he has helped clients both protect and retrieve assets involving life's savings and real estate matters. He practices solely in the areas of estate planning, estate settlement, and probate administration. Additionally, John has served as a Part-Time Magistrate Judge with the Cobb County Magistrate Court.

TABLE OF CONTENTS

DO I NEED AN ESTATE PLAN?

Before we jump into our step-by-step guide to Georgia estate planning, let's discuss whether you need an estate plan.

Everyone has an estate. Your estate includes all the things you own whether you know you own it or not. Your home, your car, your bank accounts. It also includes things like the photos on your Facebook account and your digital music collection.

You probably have some idea where you want your assets to go and when they are to go there, but good estate planning involves much more than leaving a detailed list of instructions related to your passing.

Good estate planning allows you to:

- Pass on your assets and properties to the people you want, rather than having the court decide that for you

- Appoint guardians for minor children so that you know they are in the right hands

- Prevent confusion and disputes among beneficiaries

- Provide for loved ones with special needs without interrupting their government benefits

- Provide for family members who may not be responsible with money and may need protection in the future with divorce or creditors

- Plan for disability or incapacity, including stating your preferences in end-of-life situations

- Decide how your businesses will be transferred if you are disabled or upon death

- Support a charity that you are passionate about with assets from your estate

- Continually adapt to personal, financial, and legal changes

- Reduce taxes, court fees, and legal expenses for your loved ones after you pass

An estate plan can not only preserve your lifetime's work, but also help ease the burden off of your family and minimize potential conflicts between your loved ones. Attaining peace of mind and reassurance for life's uncertainties is invaluable.

What is Estate Planning?

Estate planning is often misunderstood as something only the wealthiest of families should have. In reality, everyone in Georgia can benefit from having an estate plan, whether you have a large estate or a modest one.

And no two estate plans are alike. Modern families are anything but simple. Most households have at least a sprinkling of step-parents, biological kids, adopted kids, step children, married daughters, same sex marriages, toddlers, retirees, grandchildren and, of course, beloved pets.

While your family may not include each of the above, there's a fair chance your family contains one or more of them. For this reason, estate planning cannot be successful using a cookie-cutter approach. Each estate plan must be individualized for your particular family.

Many people believe that estate planning is about getting a Last Will and Testament in place. While that is part of it, estate planning is much more.

Estate planning begins with a Last Will and Testament and/or a Trust - the pillars of a good estate plan. You might be okay with just a Will, or you may want something more sophisticated like a Trust. But, know now that you at least need a Will.

In addition to one or both of these basic estate planning pillars, you should also have a Financial Power of Attorney and an Advance Healthcare Directive. These items cover you should you become disabled or incapacitated.

In general, a complete estate plan will contain the following documents:

- Will
- Trust
- Powers of attorney
- Beneficiary designations
- Medical directives

Already have an estate plan?

If so, good on you! Only around 40% of Americans have prepared an estate plan. If you do have an estate plan, remember that estate planning is an ongoing process. It requires regular updates as you go through major changes in life, like a relocation, divorce or a new birth.

Not only do family situations change regularly, but so do estate laws. You want to make sure that your estate plan is current, legally binding, and reflects your goals.

If you already have an estate plan, it's important to check a few things regularly to ensure your estate plan is still maximized:

Locate your estate planning documents

They are probably tucked away in a special hiding place or in a safe-deposit box at the bank. Take the time to make sure they are still there. It will also give you the opportunity to review them to make sure things will be handled exactly as you want them to be handled when you pass. If you can't find your estate planning documents, read on to learn how to ensure your legacy is secure.

Review compliance with Georgia law

If you've moved to Georgia from another state, it's important to have your estate planning documents reviewed to ensure they comply with Georgia law. While a Will made in another state is still valid, there may be elements of Georgia law that will work to your advantage. Also, if you've purchased property in Georgia, it may be necessary to include that property in your estate plans.

Update your beneficiaries

Review who you have designated as beneficiaries. Do you need to add or subtract a beneficiary? Perhaps you've named someone as a beneficiary that you no longer speak with or perhaps no longer have a business relationship with. Perhaps a child has special needs that have not been addressed in your Will or Trust.

Double check your powers of attorney

Like your beneficiary designations, you should review your powers of attorney to ensure your agent is someone you still trust to handle your financial and health decisions.

A STEP–BY–STEP GUIDE TO GEORGIA ESTATE PLANNING

To help make your estate planning experience a little easier, we have broken down the process into a several steps. By no means is this guide a complete analysis of Georgia estate planning. It is meant to be used in conjunction with the assistance of an experienced Georgia estate planning and probate attorney.

DEFINE YOUR ESTATE PLANNING GOALS

It is a good idea to begin your estate plan by identifying exactly what it is you want to accomplish. Of course, you want to make sure your property and assets are properly distributed upon your passing – but this can mean several things.

Dying without a will in Georgia means the state decides the distribution regardless of your wishes or your loved one's needs. If you die without creating a will, your estate will be passed down according to intestate laws (we discuss more about intestate laws below).

If you are married, your spouse will usually inherit your estate if you do not have children or grandchildren. If you die with a spouse and children, then they will divide your estate equally depending on the number of children you have. If you do not have a spouse or children, then your estate may pass on to your parents, siblings, or other relatives next in line to inherit according to the law.

This means even an estranged spouse from whom you've been separated for the past 5 years could inherit your assets. Without a spouse or children, your assets will go to other biological relatives (even those you have never met). If you have no heirs, then the estate may be transferred to the board of education in the county that your estate was filed.

So while dying intestate is one way to distribute your assets, it's certainly not the best way. It's better to make sure your legacy goes to those you choose yourself.

This is why a good start is to define your estate planning goals. Ask yourself a few questions:

- Do you want to choose who will raise your minor children?
- Do you want to put aside protection for your adult special needs child?
- Do you want to ensure your business enters the right hands if you become disabled or die?
- Are you interested in minimizing estate taxes, court fees and legal expenses?
- Do you need to describe your wishes for funeral arrangements and expenses?
- Do you have medical preferences for end-of-life situations?

- Is there a group or charity you wish to support upon your passing?

List the things that are important to you and refer to this list as you plan your estate.

LIST YOUR ASSETS

This step is fairly straight forward. You want to list what things of value will be left behind should you become incapacitated or pass away. This list may include:

- Real estate
- Investments
- Pension plans
- Insurance policies
- Retirement accounts
- Checking accounts
- Savings accounts
- Business interests
- Personal effects
- Valuable collectibles

...and anything else you can think of. An experienced Georgia estate planning and probate lawyer can also help you brainstorm assets you may not think of yourself.

CHOOSE YOUR BENEFICIARIES

List the individuals in your life whom you want to receive a portion of your estate upon your passing. Beneficiaries may be individuals like your spouse and children, or they can be a corporation or nonprofit organization.

Note that some beneficiaries may already be designated through other instruments. For example, certain payable-on-death bank accounts, investment accounts, retirement accounts, 401(k)s and life insurance policies require you to designate the beneficiaries and bypass probate. In addition, property owned jointly will go to the individual with right of survivorship.

PREPARE YOUR WILL

When it comes to estate planning (or the lack thereof), not having a Will, or a Last Will and Testament, in place is one of the biggest mistakes you can make and could have lasting consequences.

It has been said that more than half the people in Georgia do not have a Will in place. It is startling to think that some parents will leave more instructions to their babysitter when they are going to be gone for one night than they will leave for their family when they are going to be gone for a lifetime and will be unable to call home to check in.

We often hear these stories when it comes to celebrities. But, the fact is no matter how wealthy or poor, young or old, everyone should at least have a Will in place.

A Will is a legal document where a person, also known as a testator, states and expresses their wishes and desires as to the disposition of their property following their death. This is not to be confused with the Living Will described later relating to the Advance Directive. Instead, the Last Will and Testament is used following someone's passing rather than before their passing as with the Advance Directive.

A properly arranged will can provide:

- Your children with a guardian you appoint
- Specific instructions about how your assets are divided
- An executor of your choosing for your estate
- Assurance that your possessions go to the people you want
- A trust for any minors you name in your will

You'll want to consult with a Georgia will and estate planning attorney when drafting your Will and related documents. One of the nice things about a Will is that you are able to modify it at any time so long as you are mentally competent. You can change it if you have a change in your financial, family, or other circumstances.

Tip: Some estate planning firms like Georgia's Farrell Law Firm offer consultations free of charge.

GEORGIA LAW REGARDING VALID WILLS

Each state, including Georgia, sets the laws which govern the making and validity of Wills. While there are several different types of Wills, Georgia only allows Wills that are written. Nuncupative (oral) wills are not allowed in Georgia. As you might expect, this is where a person tells others how the property is to be distributed but doesn't commit his or her desires to paper.

Written Wills fall into two categories: holographic Wills and typewritten Wills. Holographic Wills are written entirely in the handwriting of the testator, but the most typical type of Will is typed instead of written.

State law sets the requirements for a valid Will and every state is different. In Georgia, here are the essential elements of a valid Will:

1) The person making the Will must be at least fourteen (14) years old. Imagine that. Someone who can't obtain a learner's permit to drive can make a valid Will.

2) They must be of "sound mind." Generally, this means they haven't officially been declared incompetent.

3) The Will must be written. Oral Wills are not valid.

4) The Will must be signed by the Testator (the person making the Will). Many times, my clients ask whether they should sign their full name including any middle names. Generally, I tell people to sign it how they would normally sign a document. If it becomes a question of whether it's the person's signature or not, they will compare it with the signature on other documents such as the driver's license, the back of the credit cards, or any letters written to friends.

5) The Will must be signed by two (2) witnesses.

IN TERROREM CLAUSES (THE POISON PILL)

I once had a client visit my office to discuss establishing his estate plan. Interestingly, he was 93 years old, but he didn't have an estate plan at all. He had two children, one son and one daughter, who were in their late sixties. He wanted to divide his estate between the two, but not equally. Instead, he wanted to leave 90% to the son and 10% to the daughter.

As usual, I asked follow-up questions about why he wanted to give them different percentages and how they would feel about receiving different amounts. He said he anticipated that the daughter may be upset, but he had his reasons. He knew that his daughter was well-to-do and that his son would benefit more from the inheritance than she would. But, he was concerned whether there would be a legal fight from the division of his assets in this way.

One of the more interesting things about estate planning is the different ways people can control the disposition of their property following their death. I counseled this client about adding a provision to his estate planning documents that would discourage his children from contesting his estate. It's called an In Terrorem clause, or the "poison pill" as it is known.

The Poison Pill provision discourages a beneficiary from contesting the Will or Trust by threatening to remove the inheritance if they do. Typically, the beneficiary or heir will be glad to receive something instead of potentially losing everything. Usually, in response to the harsh nature of the poison pill provision, the client will say the heir should be thankful for what they do receive and, if they are not so thankful, then the inheritance will be removed and it will be distributed amongst the other heirs or beneficiaries who do not contest the Will or Trust.

This can be a powerful mechanism to keep children from fighting over what they receive through an inheritance. As you can imagine, it typically will only work on those who actually do receive some form of an inheritance. If the person isn't scheduled to receive anything anyway, there is no incentive for the person to not contest the Will or Trust. After all, at that point, they will have nothing to lose.

SHOULD I FILE THE WILL?

This is an interesting question I get all the time. Typically, the person will tell me they are the surviving spouse and everything is passing to them. Other times, it may be an adult child who tells me mom and dad had very little or everything they had fell outside of the probate process. But, the answer to the question is always "yes" because, in Georgia, it is a crime to have or know where the Will is located and not file it the Court upon the passing of the person.

In Georgia, the law permits a Probate Judge to issue sanctions of fines and jail time if the Will is not delivered to the Court. It is classified as a misdemeanor with a fine up to $500.00 and a jail sentence not to exceed 20 days. That's reason enough to file the Will. But, there are even more reasons.

You cannot assume that assets that are titled jointly are not part of the person's estate. The reason for this is because there are different types of joint ownership. Some types pass outside of the probate process, but some pass through the probate process. Additionally, you will need to check beneficiary designations on life insurance policies and retirement accounts. Perhaps there's a problem with the designation that would cause it to pass through the probate process.

For these reasons, it is always necessary to at least file the Will with the Probate Court. But, the probate process doesn't have to be overwhelming. There are steps that can be taken during a person's lifetime that can minimize or avoid altogether the probate process.

It's important to consult with a Georgia will and estate planning attorney who has an excellent working knowledge of the practical effects of the property laws, trust code, and the probate process in drafting a complete and comprehensive Will.

WHAT HAPPENS IF I DON'T HAVE A WILL?

Interestingly, most people pass away without having an estate plan in place. It's understandable. It's a topic that a lot of people don't like talking about. Some fear the old adage, "speak of the devil and he shall appear." Unfortunately, it's coming for all of us whether we speak of it or not and it's important to put a plan in place, especially if you have small children.

Another reason many people do not have an estate plan in place is they mistakenly believe their property will simply pass to their heirs equally if they die without a Will. But, if you die without a Will in Georgia, the state will decide who gets your property according to a set of established rules regardless of your thoughts and wishes on how you want your property to be distributed.

In Georgia, and in most states, passing away without a Will is called passing away "intestate." After you pass, certain types of your property will be collected into the estate and will be distributed according to Georgia's intestacy laws.

Typically, a surviving spouse and children will receive your property, but it may not be equally. The issue can be further complicated if your spouse passes along with you in a sudden accident and your spouse did not have a Will and if you have no children. If you do have children and you and your spouse were to suddenly pass, having no estate plan in place causes the decision of who will raise your children to fall upon the court.

The following describes what Georgia law has written when it comes to people who die without a Will in Georgia:

Married with no children
If you die leaving only a spouse behind, your entire estate passes to your surviving spouse. I am no longer surprised to learn that some of my clients have outlived their children. Outliving your children can lead to some unanticipated estate planning consequences.

Example. Bill and Ann are married and had three children together. Over the years, each of those children married and had two children. Bill and Ann find themselves blessed with six grandchildren. Unfortunately, Bill and Ann, now in their late '80's, lost their three children to natural causes some time ago. However, Bill and Ann are very involved with their grandchildren and have been able to see them grow into adulthood. Some of them have even started families of their own.

Bill and Ann were savers and, over time, were able to amass quite a fortune. But, they didn't plan for the inevitable and Bill passed away without a Will. Under this scenario, Ann would inherit the entire estate and Bill's grandchildren and great-grandchildren would not receive an inheritance from Bill. (For a discussion of what could happen should Ann re-marry, see the section on Blended Families).

Married with 1-2 children

Here, your spouse would receive a portion of the estate and it would depend on whether you had one or two children. If you had one child, your spouse would receive half of your estate and your child would receive the other half. If you had two children, your spouse would receive one-third of your estate and each child would receive one-third.

Married with more than two children

In this situation, the inheritance of your spouse would be reduced to one-third and the remaining children would split the other two-thirds. The surviving spouse would not receive less than one-third in any scenario if you were to pass away without a Will.

Example. Mitt and Mary are married and have five sons. In an unfortunate skiing accident, Mitt passes away without a Will. Mary receives one-third of Mitt's estate and their five children split the other two-thirds (which is two-fifteenths oddly enough). Again, Mary would not receive less than one-third.

Married with one biological child and one adopted child

In Georgia, adopted children share the same inheritance rights as natural born children. Here, your surviving spouse would receive one-third and each child would receive one-third.

Married with one biological child, one adopted child, and one stepchild

If you have stepchildren, a Will is a must! Unfortunately, a stepchild does not share the inheritance rights of a natural born child or adopted child in Georgia. In this situation, the stepchild would not receive an inheritance from the decedent.

There are at least two ways you can protect stepchildren from disinheritance. First, you can write them into the Will (it's not enough to simply say you leave your estate to your children as the Court may not recognize your stepchildren as your children).

Second, you can create a Trust and name them as beneficiaries. Either way, if you are a stepparent or have biological children who have a stepparent, take the steps to protect their inheritance.

Unmarried with no children

Have you ever heard of the Table of Consanguinity? No? Count your blessings. In the event the Court has to start looking for people who are related to you, there's a chance they will review the Table of Consanguinity to determine who is closest to you in relationship. In fact, that is what the Table shows: degrees of relationship.

Over the years, I've had just a couple of cases where we had to look for long lost relatives. So, you start to wonder whether the First Cousin Twice Removed is closer to the deceased than the Second Cousin Once Removed.

Tip: Don't die without a Will. There are plenty of reasons to have an estate plan, but there is no good reason to be without a Will.

Having the assistance of a diligent and dedicated Georgia will and estate planning attorney can ensure that your Will is as clear as possible and your assets are given to the people you truly want to have them.

DESIGNATE AN EXECUTOR

When preparing your Will, you will need to name an "executor" (sometimes called a personal representative). You can either choose who you want to be your executor or the court will appoint one for you. Keep in mind that if the court chooses your executor, that person may not be the best person for the job. For that reason, you should carefully consider who you wish your executor to be.

Under Georgia state law, an executor must be over 18 years old and of sound mind. There are certain other restrictions on executors, including specifications around corporate executors, out-of-state executors and criminal histories, that an experienced Georgia estate planning and probate attorney can inform you about.

Typically, people choose a surviving spouse, children, or siblings to be the executor. To consider who you might choose to be your executor, let's talk about some of the things your executor may be required to do.

In general, an executor will be responsible for making sure your property is distributed properly, processing any necessary transactions, dealing with creditor claims and filing tax returns on behalf of your estate.

If you have a home, your executor may be required to maintain the upkeep of the home until the estate is settled. Your executor may be required to pay your bills from the estate and make court appearances for the estate.

With that in mind, you may want to consider someone who lives close to where the courthouse and the majority of assets are located. Having to maintain property and make court appearances or even check the mail may be difficult for someone who lives far away.

Additionally, you will want to carefully consider if a family member or members will serve as your executor. Only you know the family dynamics which may lead to someone contesting the Will or family squabbles. To that end, you will probably want to discuss the issue with the family members who will be affected by the decision.

POWERS OF ATTORNEY

Many people believe that a Last Will and Testament is all they need when it comes to estate planning. But since your Last Will and Testament covers only your affairs after death, it will do nothing for you should you become incapacitated and unable to state your desires and wishes regarding your finances during life.

One of the more important features of an estate plan is having a set of disability documents in place and assigning power of attorney. As opposed to an executor who handles your affairs after you die, a power of attorney handles your affairs while you are alive, in the event that you become incapacitated or are no longer able to care for yourself.

Because the power of attorney becomes ineffective, in other words it loses its power, following your death, a power of attorney is just as important an estate planning tool as your Last Will and Testament.

There are a range of situations in which you can grant a power of attorney:

- **Financial power of attorney**: This grants full or limited authority of your finances to a family member or friend. The agent can handle bank transactions on your behalf, buy/sell property, enter into contracts, file your tax returns, and other financial transactions.

- **Advanced directives (medical power of attorney)**: Appointing someone to make limited decisions about your health care if you are unable to do so. The individual will be in charge of speaking to the doctors on your behalf and accessing your medical records. In the Advance Directive, you will state your desires and wishes regarding the withholding or withdrawal of life support systems.

These important disability documents allow a trusted family member – perhaps a spouse if you are married or an adult child – to make important financial decisions for you, pay bills on your behalf, access your medical records, or speak to a doctor on your behalf, among other things, if you ever get to a point where you are unable to do so yourself.

If you ever get to a point where you are unable to do so yourself and you don't have a set of disability documents in place, your family will have to sue you to have you be declared incompetent. Once the judge declares you incompetent, the judge will appoint a guardian for you and the guardian is the one who will make those decisions for you.

Typically, the person appointed to serve as guardian is a family member and perhaps the person you would have chosen anyway, so it's just as important to go ahead and complete the disability documents as soon as possible.

Example – Michael and Mary have two children, Matthew and Melissa. Michael and Mary have a Last Will and Testament to cover their estate should one or both of them pass away. However, they are concerned with who would take care of them if they became disabled or incapacitated for an extended period of time. So, they sign a power of attorney naming each other as their primary agent and name Matthew as their successor agent (or "back-up) in case they are unable to take care of their own affairs.

FINANCIAL POWER OF ATTORNEY

A financial power of attorney allows you to name one or more persons (your Agent) to handle your business and financial decisions just as you would if you were able. Executing a financial power of attorney does not mean you give all of the authority to handle your affairs away to your Agent. You can still handle all of your affairs as long as you are willing and able. However, unless you limit your Agent by making the power of attorney effective at some later date, your Agent will also have the authority to handle your affairs when you execute the power of attorney while you are also handling your affairs.

Sample Power of Attorney

The Georgia legislature has created a sample power of attorney which is often referred to as the statutory power of attorney. While the statutory form can be used to create a financial power of attorney, it is not the exclusive method for creating the power of attorney.

See Appendix for a Sample ("Statutory") Georgia Statutory Power of Attorney Form created by the legislature.

It is our recommendation that you either seek legal advice in creating a power of attorney or you follow the statutory form as closely as possible. Additionally, the new statutory form, which took effect July 1, 2017, creates the ability to force third parties, such as banks and financial institutions, to accept the power of attorney as long as certain conditions are met. Additionally, the statutory form was slightly modified on July 1, 2018.

If you have not designated a financial power of attorney or durable power of attorney and become too ill to handle your affairs, the court will usually appoint a conservator.

ADVANCE DIRECTIVE FOR HEALTH CARE

If you're of a certain age, the phrase "advance directive for health care" may sound foreign to you. But, you may be familiar with the phrases "durable power of attorney for healthcare" and "living will." When you prepare an advance directive for health care, you are able to specify any important preferences you have about your medical treatment.

In most states, a living will denotes your preferences for emergency medical intervention or life-support in the event that you become mentally incapacitated or otherwise unable to communicate. In 2007, Georgia essentially merged the durable power of attorney for healthcare and living will into what is now known as the Advance Directive for Health Care. Are Living Wills and Durable Powers of

Attorney signed before 2007 still valid? Yes, if they were properly executed and have not since been revoked.

Example – In 2005, after receiving concerning news from his doctor, David decided to execute a Living Will and Durable Power of Attorney for Healthcare giving his sister Patricia the authority to make healthcare decisions for him in the event he was unable to do so himself. Five years later, in 2010, David entered the hospital for a few days, but was able to state his desires and wishes to the doctors and Patricia was never able to exercise the authority given to her by David's Durable Power of Attorney.

Example – Jerri suffered a heart attack and survived, but remained in a vegetative state on life support systems following the occurrence. Because she did not have a Living Will in place, it was unclear whether she wanted to remain on life support or not. Her family differed on what they believed her wishes and desires were relating to the withholding or withdrawal of those life support systems. As a consequence, she remained on life support for many years while the courts considered arguments from the family as to Jerri's wishes and desires.

In my experience, this is the document which takes the most time to complete when my clients are in the office to sign their documents at an event I call the "final signing meeting." I believe it is the most time-consuming portion of the final signing meeting because the clients have to consider what they want done related to healthcare should they become disabled. Their passing is lightyears away to them, but the potential of becoming disabled is much more real to them. Deciding now whether they want to be taken off life support if something were to happen to them is something they'd rather put off than face. Most of them do not fear death, but many of them fear being on life support.

Interestingly, whether to be put on life support or not is not a decision that is uniform amongst my clients. It's easy to say that 50 percent of them would rather not be put on life support and 50 percent do want to be put on life support. Either way, the decision is right because it is your decision.

See Appendix for a Georgia Advance Directive for Health Care Form created by the legislature.

An experienced Georgia estate planning and probate lawyer can help ensure that your power of attorney is properly granted to the person you want to be in charge of your affairs.

MINIMIZE TAXES

"Tis impossible to be sure of anything but Death and Taxes" –
Christopher Bullock (1716)

Most people who are concerned with "death" taxes lump the estate tax and the inheritance tax together. But, they are distinct and it's easy to distinguish them by who pays the tax. The estate tax, for example, is paid by the estate of the person who passed away. The inheritance tax, however, is paid by the person who receives an inheritance. But, there are also other types of taxes that you should be concerned with when planning your estate, such as the capital gains tax.

ESTATE TAXES

For many years, Georgia residents were subject to an estate tax, but it was based upon the federal estate tax. In 2005, Congress phased out the portion related to state estate taxes, so Georgia stopped collecting estate taxes. It was always a possibility that those taxes based upon the federal tax could come back, so Georgia, in 2014, decided to eliminate the estate tax altogether. So, for those in Georgia whose date of death is after 2014, there is no concern that a state estate tax will need to be paid.

However, there is a federal estate tax. This tax applies to estates of those people who were residents of any state when they passed away. However, there is an exemption amount which varies each year. In other words, if the estate is valued at less than the exemption amount, then no federal estate tax is owed.

The way it works, as you can imagine, is the assets of the deceased are added up. These include things like the home, bank accounts, retirement accounts, business interests, etc. If the value of those assets are above the exemption amount, then the value above the exemption amount is taxed fairly heavily, as much as 40%.

The federal exemption amount was relatively low for many years which means many estates were subject to federal estate tax. Thus, a lot of estate planning around the time focused on minimizing or eliminating the estate tax. Over time, the exemption was raised and adjusted for inflation and reached as high as $5,490,000 causing fewer and fewer estates to be subject to the federal estate tax.

In 2017, President Trump signed a bill enacted by Congress which doubled the current exemption rate to $10,980,000 which was then adjusted for inflation and raised to $11,200,000. Thus, very few Americans need to worry about the federal estate tax these days.

Further, surviving spouses are able to take advantage of the unused exemption of the deceased spouse under something called "portability." So, a surviving spouse could increase his or her exemption by the amount of the unused exemption of the deceased spouse.

Example. Mitch dies in 2018 with an estate valued at $6,000,000. This value is deducted from the exemption amount (currently

$11,200,000) leaving an unused exemption of $5,200,000. If the tax paperwork is prepared correctly, the estate tax exemption of Mitch's spouse will be increased to $16,400,000. So, as long as the estate of Mitch's spouse is below $16,400,000, no federal estate tax will be owed by Mitch or his spouse upon their passing.

Pro tip: Being able to "port" the unused exemption is critical to increasing the exemption of the surviving spouse, so make sure you consult an experienced Georgia Will and Estate Planning Attorney or an accountant to take advantage of this massive opportunity to minimize federal estate taxes.

Most people are concerned with minimizing or avoiding the estate tax when they pass, but with Georgia eliminating the estate tax on the state level and the exemption being so high on the federal level, most people's families will not face the estate tax upon the passing of a loved one. However, the tax most people should be concerned with is capital gains tax.

CAPITAL GAINS TAX

The capital gains tax is paid when an asset that has appreciated in value is sold. As an example, a person who bought an asset for $25,000 and then later sold that asset for $75,000 will have $50,000 in gain and will pay tax on this "capital gain." The $25,000 the person paid for the asset is called the asset's "basis."

Two terms you need to be concerned with are called "step-up in basis" and "carryover basis." When the asset is transferred to someone else, perhaps your children, which basis they are required to use has a significant impact on the capital gains tax they may be required to pay.

If you choose to allow your heirs to inherit your assets (instead of giving it to them while you are still alive), they will be allowed to use a step-up in basis. In other words, the basis will be the value of the asset upon your death instead of the value when you bought the asset.

Example. Mary purchased stock in Apple many years ago at a cost of $25,000. After having lived a long and good life, Mary passed way leaving the stock to her only child, James. When she passed away, the stock was valued at $150,000. Having received the stock as an inheritance, James received a step-up in basis. In other words, the basis upon which the capital gains tax is calculated is $150,000 and not $25,000. If James sells the stock for $150,000 shortly after Mary's passing, he will not pay a capital gains tax as a result of the sale.

However, many parents approach me and ask why they shouldn't go ahead and give their assets away before they pass. They reason that they can avoid the probate process if they divulge themselves of all of their assets before they pass away. But, the problem with this thinking is the person's heirs will receive a "carryover basis" and not the step-up in basis.

Example. As in the situation above, Mary purchased stock in Apple at a cost of $25,000. Just before her passing, she gave her only child, James, the stock which had a then current value of $150,000. Instead of James receiving a step-up in basis where he'd be able to sell the stock at $150,000 and receive no capital gains tax, he will have to deduct the original basis from the sale amount and incur a capital gains tax on the gain of $125,000.

Working with a competent Georgia estate planning and probate attorney can help ensure you are taking the right steps to minimize taxes, court fees and legal expenses for your loved ones after you pass.

PROTECT YOUR ASSETS

*"I have enough money for the rest of my life
and enough to leave a good inheritance for our kids." – David
A. Siegel*

Sometimes it becomes necessary to have a discussion with a client regarding the protection of their assets so that they can leave an inheritance for their children. Often times, they just don't consider how easy it may be to lose those assets. Typically, the person is involved in some type of business venture and they haven't taken the steps to shield themselves from the liabilities that those business ventures bring. Other times, the person may be involved in a high-risk profession such as a doctor or lawyer.

Example. Christina is unmarried and doesn't have any kids. She has an interest in real estate and uses her disposable income to purchase homes and turn them into rental properties. In addition to the seven rental properties she accumulated, she has a variety of financial investments in stocks and, over time, she has amassed a considerable net worth.

Unwittingly, she set herself up for a potential disaster. When she purchased the rental properties, she purchased them in her personal name and not in the name of a business. Therefore, if someone were to slip and fall at one of her rental properties, her other rental properties along with her personal fortune are susceptible to liability resulting from litigation involving the injury.

This is a very characteristic example of where someone hasn't considered the potential outcomes of failing to shield their net worth from potential lawsuits. Typically, people who own their own business will have incorporated the business and kept up with the corporate formalities in order have liability protection. It's not often that I see them failing to keep proper records relating to the business. From time to time, however, there will be glaring omission from their paperwork that suggests they need to get things in order.

The bottom line here is, if you have your own business, make sure you are keeping up with the proper corporate formalities or you may not have anything to leave your children should you become subject to a devastating lawsuit.

I see this most often from my clients who have rental properties. If you have a rental property, that property should be in the name of an LLC or other business. It should not be in your individual name. Otherwise, you will make your personal residence subject to a lawsuit relative to the rental property.

Levels of protection

There are different levels when it comes to asset protection and, of course, each plan will depend on the circumstances of the client. One of the most basic levels of protection involves taking advantage of whatever exemptions may apply to your situation.

Example. Richard and Lucille have been married for many years and live in an apartment in New York. Richard is a talented singer and makes a respectable living leading a band. He takes the vast majority of his earnings and places them in a 401(k) and life insurance policies. Later, Richard is sued by an unhappy customer.

The customer says that Richard's work as a bandleader is so bad that the customer is no longer able to enjoy good music. After obtaining a sizeable judgment against Richard, the customer is further disgruntled when he learns that 401(k)'s and life insurance policies are generally exempt from the hands of creditors. Because of the nature of Richard's holdings, his assets are protected from the customer.

The bottom line is that certain financial instruments may be protected by either state or federal law. Here, a good Georgia will and estate planning attorney can help you discover where you are protected and where you are open to liability.

Another level of protection involves creating and maintaining proper business entities. As in the case above with the young lady who owned the many rental properties, it may be necessary to place the ownership of that asset into a business. One of the more popular business forms for liability protection is the Limited Liability Company, or the LLC for short.

The LLC allows for, as the name suggests, limited liability for the members or owners. Additionally, the requirements to maintain the corporate status aren't as rigid as with a normal corporation. The better protection from liability and the easier to maintain corporate formalities makes the LLC a go-to business model for asset protection.

But, perhaps you are a professional such as a doctor or lawyer. Many states offer PLLC's or Professional Limited Liability Company. In fact, some states limit the types of business entity depending on the profession. Some make you choose between the PLLC and a PC, or Professional Corporation.

Also, the entity choice requirement isn't just limited to doctors and lawyers. Many states require or suggest professionals such as accountants, architects, dentists, land surveyors, veterinarians, or even harbor pilots, be incorporated as a certain business entity.

Obviously, if you are a professional and you need to incorporate, I can't stress the importance enough of retaining a Georgia business or estate planning attorney to help you. Creating, keeping, and maintaining proper corporate formalities is key to obtaining limited liability from potential loss of assets.

A higher level of protection involves creating a Domestic Asset Protection Trust, or DAPT.

DON'T FORGET DIGITAL ASSETS

There was a time not long ago when Digital Assets simply weren't a concern because they didn't exist. But, everyday, the number of people who own Digital Assets, whether they know it or not, continues to grow. Consider this – there's a fair chance you have a Facebook account. You may also have a personal email account through someone like Google or Yahoo.

You may store your photographs on a website such as Snapfish. Do you have ebooks on a Kindle or through Amazon? What about electronic music? Would you happen to have a digital currency like Bitcoin or Ethereum? These are just small examples of the types of Digital Assets you might own.

Many people don't consider that they should take steps to make sure these digital assets are passed on following their death, but their children do. I came to realize the importance of this through a personal story.

The brother of a friend of mine passed away untimely. A few months later on the birthday of the brother, the family received emails and notices through social media that they should wish the brother a happy birthday. The family will receive a reminder every year for the rest of their lives that their brother is no longer with them. Of course, they will never forget their brother, but it's a sober reminder that our lives may live on through social media unless steps are taken to pass along these important assets to our families.

Make a list

This is an obvious choice, but I would be surprised if you could write down all of your digital assets in one sitting. More than likely, you'll be able to list most of your digital assets and then will come back from time to time to add new ones or ones you simply forgot you had. But, the most important thing is to simply start. When you make this list, remember to write down how to access them.

Decide on distribution

Once you make the list, decide what you want to do with the Digital Assets. For some, such as pictures and music, you may simply want to give them to your family. For others, such as revenue-generating assets such as an online store or accounts that have "points" or "credits," do you want those to be managed or shut down and sold? An experienced Georgia estate planning attorney can assist you in making those decisions.

Choose a representative

Now, consider who is going to follow your wishes. It may be your Executor or Trustee. It may be that grandchild who is computer savvy. Either way, it's a very important decision. Again, a good Georgia estate planning attorney can assist you in this decision.

MINOR CHILDREN

"Enough money so that they would feel they could do anything, but not so much that they could do nothing." –
Warren Buffett, when asked how much money should be left to children.

Many people, if not most, engage in estate planning because they want to provide an inheritance, or a legacy, to their children and grandchildren. This group of people will often include parents, grandparents, aunts, uncles, siblings, and sometimes good friends who simply want to leave something to a beloved young person in the family.

Some of their concerns include:

- Ensuring that the right person raises their children if something were to happen to them.

- They have a son-in-law or daughter-in-law that they hope will not squander their child's inheritance.

- Their child is not savvy either financially or socially and the parent suspects the child will blow through the inheritance quickly to their detriment.

Fortunately, there are things you can do to protect the inheritance you plan to leave to minor children. Let's talk about some of the common mistakes people make or some of the misconceptions they have when it comes to leaving an inheritance for minor children.

Many parents believe that if they leave a Will and name a guardian in that Will for the minor children that the guardian will be able to automatically use the inheritance to take care of the children. It's unfortunate that it just isn't so.

First, the Will is probated with the Probate Court. Typically, this is done several weeks or months after the person has passed away. (This is also why you don't want to put funeral arrangements in the Will. By the time anyone gets around to reading the Will, the funeral has long passed).

An important thing to consider is that your guardian will not become the guardian of your minor children simply because you have passed away. Instead, the Court will appoint a guardian. Almost always, the guardian will be the person who you've named in the Will, but not always. The Court has discretion to appoint a guardian in the minor's best interest, but great, great deference is given to who the parents want the guardian to be.

Once the Court appoints the guardian, it is the Court, and not the guardian, who will control the inheritance until the child reaches 18. While the guardian will be able to use some of the inheritance, the guardian will be heavily supervised by the Court. Then, once the child reaches 18, the child will receive the inheritance in a lump sum. This isn't ideal to some parents, but it is what happens if you have a simple Will naming a guardian for your minor children.

Additionally, this process of the Court appointing a guardian is often a time-consuming and expensive one. Every expense must be well-documented and approved by the Court. All of these expenses are paid out of the inheritance and the Court attempts to treat everyone equally so it may be difficult to manage each child's special requirements and needs.

So, how do you provide the inheritance for the minor children? The best option to provide an inheritance for a minor child is through a trust.

However, and this is a big however, if you have minor children, you must have a Will. It's an absolute. Having a Last Will and Testament is the only way you can name a guardian for your children and you absolutely want to name a guardian for your minor children. If you don't, the Court will decide who raises your children should something happen to you.

Don't fall into the misconception that you don't have enough to warrant having a Last Will and Testament. If you have minor children, you have everything. Get a Will.

ALL THE LITTLE THINGS

HANDLE YOUR PERSONAL EFFECTS

Years ago, people used to put the disposition of their personal effects into their Will. These include things like clothing, jewelry, furniture, art, tools, dishes and flatware, etc. All of those non-titled things you may have sitting in your home. But, we as practitioners realized that every time someone changed their mind about who should get the furniture we would have to prepare a Codicil to the Will and go through the same formalities of executing a Will to effect the change. Over time, we realized there was a better way.

These days, we prepare something called a Personal Property Memorandum or an Estate Planning Letter. In this memo or letter, you can provide a list of the personal effects that you have and who you want to get them. Then, if you change your mind, you can simply write in the memorandum yourself who now gets the furniture without going through all of the formalities as you would if you were changing your Will.

You can reference in the Will that there may be a separate document than the Will (the Personal Property Memorandum) that will dispose of the personal effects. But, if there is a conflict, know that the Will takes precedence.

While this method of disposing of personal effects works really well, if you feel there might be an issue with a particular item (maybe you have two daughters, but only one tennis bracelet), then you should note in the Will who is getting the item.

MAKE FUNERAL ARRANGEMENTS

You don't want to include your funeral arrangements in your Will because the funeral will be over by the time anyone gets around to reading it. But, there is a possibility to include a section in your papers where you describe your funeral arrangement requests.

As a side note, we include a Portfolio for our clients that have tabs for the different estate planning documents. That way, we can tell clients to tell their family to simply find the Portfolio if something happens to them. Then, they can turn to the tab called "Memorial Instructions" for funeral requests.

In the paperwork, you can explain whether you want the funeral to be for friends and relatives or whether you'd prefer it to be private. List any burial plots you may own and any end-of-life wishes regarding organ donation, burial or cremation. You can also explain any religious beliefs or memberships you may be involved with.

Additionally, you can describe any scripture and music selections you may wish to include. Again, it's just another opportunity to make things simple on the family when you're no longer here.

ORGANIZE YOUR DOCUMENTS

While most of us aren't as organized as we would like to be, it's important to maintain a system that can help you and your loved ones find your estate planning documents whenever the need arises.

Problems with a disorganized estate plan happen more often than you would think.

Unable to find the original Will

"I've set things up so that my family can take the Will to the Courthouse, file it, and the probate will be simple." I've heard this one a number of times only to have the family at my conference room table pulling their hair out because they can't find the original Will.

"He told us he had a Will, but we've turned his house upside down and we can't find it." As part of my New Year's resolution recommendations, I tell people to find their estate planning documents to ensure they are still in the same place. Make sure your family knows where you keep the original Will and don't assume they'll simply be able to find it once you pass.

We only have a copy of the Will

"We couldn't find the original Will, but we did find a copy." This is problematic because the Court will presume that you wanted to revoke the Will if the family can only produce a photocopy of the Will. After all, the Court presumes, if you wanted the disposition of your assets as outlined in the photocopy to be done, you would have made sure the family had the original Will. Again, make sure you have the original Will and that your family is able to find it.

There is no Self-Proving Affidavit with the Will

"Thank goodness we were able to find the original Will because now everything will be so easy!" Not so fast. From time to time, families will bring me the original Will without the Self-Proving Affidavit. The Self-Proving Affidavit allows your family to file the Will without the need to contact the witnesses to the Will.

Without the Self-Proving Affidavit, your family will need to track down the people who witnessed the signing of your Will and, if they are actually able to find them, pray they will be cooperative enough to fill out a 10 question Interrogatory in the presence of a Notary, all the while spending time and money so they can move the probate of your Will forward.

If you've taken the time and expense to create a Will, make sure you complete a Self-Proving Affidavit and, again, make sure your Family will be able to find the original of both.

This is just a sampling of the issues that families have to face when things don't go perfectly. Make sure to have your estate plan reviewed every year or two by an experienced Georgia estate planning attorney and take the steps to ensure your family will be able to find the originals of your estate plans.

Keep track of trust assets

One of the major complaints that I hear from family members following a loved one's passing is that it took them forever to figure out what mom or dad had. Typically, they say they have to monitor the mail for all of the bills to come through before they can make a final determination about the family's assets.

To make it easier on the family, you should keep track and provide proof of every asset that you have or that has been transferred to a trust.

Keep a running list of your trust assets with all of your other estate planning documents. Again, since your estate planning documents are not "set it and forget it," you should review this list annually to make sure nothing has been transferred out or transferred in that is not on the list. As a general rule, our firm provides a section in the Portfolio for you to make such a list. Again, this is just something that will make it easier on the family when that day comes (and it will come for all of us).

Here is a sampling of some of the things you will want to include on this list:

- **Real estate:** The legal description is very handy to have, but if you transferred the real estate to the trust, then the deed doing so should be kept with the list. If you don't have a copy of the deed to the property to include with the list, definitely include the address of the property. Obviously, this goes for real estate no matter where it is located, whether in your state of residence, another state, or another country.

- **Bank accounts:** You'd be surprised how often this comes up. Typically, the family will have some general idea of where you bank, but they may be unaware of how many accounts you have, whether checking or saving or otherwise, and if you have bank accounts at multiple places. It's a good idea to also list the account numbers associated with these accounts.

- **Investments:** This is probably obvious to you, but be sure to include any investment accounts in this list.

- **Beneficiary designations:** Absolutely list the insurance policies or other assets which have beneficiary designations and who those beneficiary designations are. If you have stock certificates, be sure to include a photocopy of those with your estate planning documents.

- **Vehicles:** List any vehicles you may own on the list. Included with this list, you should keep copies of any titles to vehicles you have, or the original title if you happen to own the vehicle free and clear.

- **Other important items:** You should also include a list of any debts that you have. Include things like credit card bills, etc. Additionally, include a list of where everything is located. For example, you may keep your original Will in a safe place. Be sure to include where that safe place is located.

Additionally, there are other estate planning vehicles you can use to make it easy on your family when you're no longer here. An experienced Georgia estate planning attorney can help tailor your estate plan to meet your specific needs.

MAINTAIN UPDATED MATERIALS

There is an old saying that the only constant thing in this world is change. Unfortunately, estate planning, Wills included, is not something you can "set and forget." Life comes at you fast and things change before you realize it. I always recommend to my clients they have their estate plan updated whenever there has been (1) a change in the law or (2) a change in their family circumstances.

Knowing when there are changes in the law is of course a bit difficult for clients because, rightfully so, they don't sit around waiting for the latest Supreme Court case to be handed down or keep track of legislation going through the state capital like we lawyers do.

But, every year, there are minor shifts in the law and sometimes there are major ones.

Example – Jimmy and Mildred have been married for many years. Through hard work, they have amassed a fortune they wish to pass down to their three children when they are no longer here. Through their estate planning attorney, they have designed a plan that will substantially reduce the estate taxes they will pay once they pass away.

They understand that a certain amount of their wealth is exempt from estate taxes. Then, the IRS announces, as it does every year, that the amount which is exempted will change. After all, they adjust the exemption with inflation. As a consequence, Jimmy and Mildred will need to adjust their estate plan to maximize the benefits of the exemption.

A few years ago, the U.S. Supreme Court issued a ruling in *Obergefell v. Hodges* declaring that state bans on same-sex marriage are unconstitutional. Before this, estate planning lawyers had to be creative to help same-sex couples with their estate planning. Now, with the options wide open, same-sex couples should revisit their estate plans and have them updated.

In July 2017, Georgia's Uniform Power of Attorney Act became effective. This Act is designed, among other things, to force third parties, such as banks, to accept and honor a power of attorney. Additionally, it is designed to protect people from bad agents who misuse the power of attorney and try to hurt the people they are supposed to help.

Powers of attorney which were created prior to July 1, 2017 will continue to be valid if they were valid at the time they were executed. But, if you have one that was created before July 1, 2017, it is a good idea to execute a new one especially if the power of attorney is more than a few years old. Updating your power of attorney will also make it more likely that the bank will honor it since the banks will be more familiar with the new forms as time goes on.

Changes in the law can also occur if you relocate to a new state. If you've recently moved to Georgia, your Will from another state is still valid, but there may be some statutes that you can take advantage of as a Georgia resident.

Congress, the state legislature, and the courts are constantly rewriting the playbook. What worked for you last year may not work for you this year.

Additionally, your family circumstances will change. Loved ones will pass away and new ones will be born into this world. Your children may marry and, soon enough, you may find yourself as a grandparent when it seemed you were changing the diapers of your children just a few short years ago. As your family changes, so will your needs and your goals.

Example. Danny and Claire are preparing to celebrate their 25th wedding anniversary by taking a trip overseas. They've been very fortunate to have four children. The phone rings and their daughter tells them her long-term boyfriend just proposed and she accepted. Instead of planning their anniversary, they now prepare for their daughter's wedding. When they hang up the phone, it rings again. This time, it's their son.

He tells them his wife is pregnant with their first child and they, the parents, will now be grandparents. Still reeling from the first two phone calls, they hang up the phone and it rings again. Now, the other son is on the line and said he decided to drop out of college and use his savings to become co-partners in a business with a Prince from Nigeria. Realizing their son may be moving back home, they hang up the phone and it rings again. This time, they let it go to voice-mail.

Perhaps you've had an addition to the family, such as a new daughter or a new grandson. Perhaps you've lost someone in the family. Perhaps you've moved. Perhaps those you've designated as agents in a power-of-attorney are no longer that close to you. Perhaps you're concerned with an over-controlling daughter-in-law or a not-quite-perfect son-in-law. These are just a few of the family circumstances which may warrant having your estate planning documents updated or reviewed.

Estate planning is not "set-it-and-forget it." Changes in your family circumstances or changes in the law can change the effectiveness or intent of your estate planning.

How often should you review your estate plan? A good rule of thumb is:

Once a year

Give your Will a quick review, updating it with births, marriages, divorces, deaths, new property and new beneficiary designations.

Don't forget to review beneficiary designations on things like retirement accounts, 401(k)s, annuities and life insurance policies are something you should review from time to time. It's an important point to remember that, on accounts like these, the beneficiary designation will control who gets the proceeds - not your Will or Trust.

Once every two to five years

Have your Georgia estate planning attorney review your estate planning documents to ensure your plan is still maximized according to current law.

Be sure to select a Georgia estate planning and probate attorney who offers **free-of-charge** consultations to your estate planning documents.

THE PROBATE PROCESS

An informative guide on Georgia estate planning wouldn't be complete without a discussion of the probate process. "Probate" is the process of transferring the assets from one who has passed away to either the heirs (also called "beneficiaries") as named in the Will or the heirs as determined by the law when there is no Will.

When you pass away, your family may need to visit a probate court in order to claim their inheritance. This can happen if you own property (like a house, car, bank account, investment account, or other asset) in only your name.

Although having a will is a good basic form of planning, a will does *not* avoid probate. Instead, a will simply allows you to inform the probate court of your wishes - your family still has to go through the probate process to make those wishes legal.

Typically, the family will gather the Will and any information they have about their loved one's assets and debts and visit an attorney. The attorney will prepare and file a variety of documents with the Court and the Court should ultimately file an Order giving Letters Testamentary to the Executor. Letters Testamentary is the document which gives the Executor the authority to do what he or she needs to do relative to the Estate of the deceased loved one. As you can imagine, this takes time.

The more information the family can gather about the deceased, the easier it will be to file the appropriate paperwork with the Court. Just some of the information the family should gather includes:

- Bank statements

- Titles to real estate

- Credit card statements

- Medical bills

- Investment accounts

- Titles to vehicles

- Funeral expenses

- Last Will and Testament (if there is one)

Generally, there are two types of probate: domiciliary and ancillary. Most probates are domiciliary, but some are both domiciliary and ancillary.

Domiciliary Probate

This is a probate filed in the county of residence of the decedent. Every probate should be domiciliary probate. Most of the time, this isn't complicated. Determine where the person lived at the time of their death and file the Will in that County's Probate Court.

Ancillary Probate

Once the domiciliary probate is filed, it may be necessary to resolve the status of assets owned by the decedent that are located in a different county or state. If so, an ancillary probate will need to be filed.

Typically, the Probate Court in the county where the property is located is notified that a Probate case has been filed in the other county and that the ancillary probate is necessary to give the property to the heirs.

Example – Mary owned a home in Cobb County, Georgia, where she resided. But she also owned a condominium unit, a vacation home if you will, in Panama City Beach, Florida. She, her children, and her grandchildren always enjoyed visiting the white, sandy beaches for some vacation time.

Mary had a Last Will and Testament leaving her Cobb County home and her vacation home to her children equally. So, her children filed a domiciliary probate in Cobb County and then filed an ancillary probate in Panama City Beach, Florida. The domiciliary probate takes care of her assets in Cobb County (where she resided and where all of her assets are located with the exception of the condominium unit) and the ancillary probate takes care of the condominium unit in Florida, which is the only asset located outside of Cobb County.

Pro Tip: As you can see, this can become quite time-consuming and costly. Filing one probate is bad enough, but now having to file two probates? Imagine if she also owned a cabin in Tennessee and now had to do three probates!!

STEPS IN THE GEORGIA PROBATE PROCESS

Probate can be a confusing and time-consuming process that many families would rather avoid. While probate is not always necessary, it is common for families to undergo probate if the deceased owned assets solely in his or her name and there is a great deal of uncertainty on how to divvy up the assets.

The Georgia probate process usually involves:

- Finding the deceased's will
- Filing the will with the probate court
- Creating an inventory of the deceased's assets and debts and filing this with the court
- Paying off the deceased's debts
- Publishing a notice to creditors in the local newspaper
- Filing tax returns for the estate
- Distributing the remaining assets to beneficiaries of the estate

The probate process can be full of obstacles. For many people, probate disputes can be emotional and hard to quickly resolve. It is helpful to have a seasoned Georgia estate planning and probate lawyer to assist you in navigating the complex laws and rules of probate. Your lawyer can also help you resolve disputes in mediation or in the court.

3 REASONS YOU WANT TO AVOID PROBATE

As mentioned above, many families would like to avoid the probate process if at all possible. There are several reasons for this.

1. It is all public record

Almost everything that goes through the courts, including probate, becomes a matter of public record. This means when your estate goes through probate, all associated family and financial information becomes accessible to anyone who wants to see it.

This doesn't necessarily mean account numbers and social security numbers, since the courts have at least taken some steps to reduce the risk of identity theft. But, what it does mean is that the value of your assets, creditor claims, the identities of your beneficiaries, and even any family disagreements that affect the distribution of your estate will be available, often only a click away because many courts have moved to online systems.

Most people prefer to keep this type of information private, and the best way to ensure discreteness is to keep your estate out of probate.

2. It can be expensive

Thanks to court costs, attorney fees, executor fees, and other related expenses, the price tag for probate can easily reach into the thousands of dollars, even for small or "simple" estates. These costs can easily skyrocket into the tens of thousands or more if family disputes or creditor claims arise during the process.

The money from your estate should be going to your beneficiaries, but if it goes through probate, a significant portion could go to the courts, creditors, and legal fees, instead.

Of course, setting up an estate plan that avoids probate does have its own costs. Benjamin Franklin wrote, "an ounce of prevention is worth a pound of cure." Like the "ounce of prevention," the costs you incur to put a plan in place are more easily controlled than any uncertain future costs will be - especially when you consider your family will be trying to make decisions while grieving.

With proper planning, you can avoid probate, which can minimize the risk of conflict and reduce or eliminate certain costs like court costs and executor fees. If there's no probate case there won't be any probate costs.

3. It can take some time

While the time frame for probating an estate can vary widely from county to county and by the size of the estate itself, probate is generally a lengthy process. It's not unusual for estates, even seemingly simple or small ones, to be held up in probate for 6 months to a year or more, during which time your beneficiaries may not have easy access to funds or assets.

This delay can be especially difficult on family members going through a hardship who might benefit from a faster, simpler process, such as the living trust administration process.

Bypassing probate can significantly speed the disbursement of assets, so beneficiaries can benefit sooner from their inheritance.

If your assets are located in multiple states, *the probate process must be repeated in each state in which you hold property*. This repetition can cost your family even more time and money.

The good news is that with proper trust-centered estate planning, you can avoid probate for your estate, simplify the transfer of your financial legacy, and provide lifelong asset and tax protection to your family.

ASSETS THAT AVOID THE PROBATE PROCESS

Certain assets automatically avoid the probate process. You are probably very familiar with these assets. They include things such as retirement accounts, 401(k)s, annuities and life insurance policies.

Typically, you will have already designated a beneficiary on these types of assets.

On accounts like these, most people will assign their spouse, children, or both as beneficiaries.

A classic example of where this could go wrong is where a husband names his spouse as a beneficiary to his life insurance policy and then later remarries. Perhaps he never changes the designation and, when he passes, the policy proceeds go to his new spouse and not to his children as he may have liked. Had he reviewed his beneficiary designation, he may have changed it to his children from his previous spouse.

This is a further example of how the beneficiary designation will take precedence over what is written in a Will. Imagine if he had changed his Will before his second marriage thinking those proceeds would go to his children.

Here is an additional concern to think about. If you want to have some certainty about who gets the proceeds of your life insurance policy, perhaps consider naming a trust as the primary beneficiary of the policy. If you simply leave the proceeds to a named individual, such as a spouse, it's quite possible that named individual takes the proceeds and leaves them to someone you don't know (such as a new spouse) following their passing. In other words, if you want to ensure your children receive some benefit from the proceeds, perhaps consider using a trust.

Pro Tip: In Georgia, you can even have real estate avoid the probate process through Joint Tenancy with Rights of Survivorship

("JTROS"). But know that with blended families, JTROS can be a ticking time bomb.

Example. Augustine and Mary had six children. They wanted their estate to be simple. What they really wanted was the surviving spouse to get all of the assets when the first spouse died. And, then, when the surviving spouse died, they wanted their assets to be divided equally amongst their six children.

They had their home deeded with rights of survivorship with each other so that, when one spouse died, the surviving spouse would receive the deceased spouse's interest in the home. In other words, the surviving spouse would receive full title to the home without having to probate a Will. In fact, when Augustine later died, Mary received his interest in the home and now owned the full title to the home.

As often happens, Mary decided to remarry. Because it was simple when Augustine had passed away, they deeded the home to each other with rights of survivorship. Unfortunately, Mary predeceased her new husband and he received full title to the home. He then left his estate, which included the home, to the children from his previous marriage effectively disinheriting the children of Augustine and Mary.

Sometimes, people have the best of intentions. But, they don't take the steps to ensure their wishes are followed through.

Example. Josiah and Anne had 7 children together. Josiah and Anne divorce and he later marries Abiah. Abiah already had 10 children from a previous marriage. Josiah loves the relationship he has with Abiah and wants to take care of her and his original 7 children. So, he writes a Will leaving his estate to Abiah, but if she passes before him, his estate goes equally to his 7 children.

Josiah passes away and Abiah receives his entire estate. Abiah then leaves her estate, which now includes Josiah's, to her 10 children and Josiah's original 7 children receive nothing. (As a tip, Josiah could have established a plan that protected both his new wife and his original 7 children).

Oddly enough, I had a professor in law school who said "stepparent" is another word for "lawsuit." But, it doesn't have to be that way. With guidance from an experienced Georgia estate planning attorney, you can set up a plan that ensures your wishes are fulfilled.

DO I NEED A TRUST?

When people come into my office, the first question I ask is, "What prompted you to want to get your affairs in order?"

I get a lot of different answers to that question. Some folks just want to make their estate settlement simple for their loved ones. Others want to bypass the probate process, avoid nursing home poverty or minimize estate taxes.

Some want to make their children's inheritance divorce-proof. Some couples are concerned because they are in a second-marriage situation. There is an endless list of valid concerns that people have when it comes to getting their estate in order.

The key to a successful estate plan is choosing the right tools, and then using those tools to customize the plan toward your specific needs.

For some families, a Last Will and Testament and disability documents may be all you need in your estate plan (typically young adults with very young children). To learn more about Wills and how to create a Will that meets your specific needs, contact a seasoned estate planning attorney who will be able to guide you through the process.

However, most older families who have teen or adult children fare best with a slightly more advanced, multifaceted estate plan.

One of the primary vehicles we use these days is a trust. Trusts offer many benefits and can be a great way to protect your estate and provide for your loved ones. Setting up a trust can enable you to:

- Prevent delays and costs associated with probate

- Keep your estate settlement private

- Minimize estate taxes

- Dictate the terms of asset distribution

- Shield assets from creditors and lawsuits

- Provide for step children

- Gift biological children different amounts

- Set aside funds and a guardian for your pets

- Prevent disputes among beneficiaries

- Provide for special needs loved ones without interrupting government benefits

- Protect financially irresponsible loved ones from spending inheritance too quickly or losing it to divorce or creditors

- Prevent a son-in-law or daughter-in-law from squandering your child's inheritance

- Reduce taxes, court fees, and legal expenses for your loved ones

- Prevent nursing home poverty

- Support a charity that you are passionate about

A major reason trusts are so popular today is that they allow you to bypass the probate process required to carry out the terms of a Will.

Why do people want to avoid probate? The typical answer is, it is often a lengthy, stressful process and expenses can run high.

While all probates are different, every probate takes between several months and several years to complete. Probate often involves multiple court filings. Every time a document gets filed it must be stamped, undergo review by a law clerk, get signed by a judge, and go back through the processing department before it is finally available for the family. Those things take time.

On top of that, there is the potential for attorney delays, courthouse delays, paperwork processing delays, financial institution delays, and delays from other title companies that may be involved.

Not everyone involved in the probate process is going to be proactive. If there is one party that is not in complete agreement with how the process is going, they can file what Georgia state law refers to as a "caveat," which will basically shut down the probate process until court hearings can happen and a judge can make a decision and force the probate forward.

Regarding cost, again every probate is different —different heirs, different issues, different underlying assets, different complexities – but once you factor in things like court costs, attorneys' fees, executor compensation and other miscellaneous costs, probate can range anywhere from $3,500 to $15,000 - or more.

If you happen to be a married couple, you may have to go through the probate process twice – once when the first spouse dies and again when the second spouse dies. If you happen to own property in another state, you may have to go through it three times.

I can tell you this. When anyone has to go through the probate process, they unfortunately never leave happy. It's something that nobody wants to go through.

While a Will can help you navigate the probate process, trusts are often designed to avoid the probate process altogether. A Will goes into effect only after the person who makes the Will (the "testator") dies and it is formally recognized by the Court. On the other hand, many trusts go into effect the moment they are signed. When done right, a trust means your loved ones receive their inheritance immediately upon your passing, at no extra cost.

Another reason you may want to incorporate a trust into your estate plan is because you are a private person. Perhaps you don't want the public to know what you have and who is getting it. When a Will is filed with the Court upon your passing, it becomes available to the public. Trusts can help you keep your family's business private.

Consider the story of the mother who left her daughter an inheritance of jewelry and furs. The Will was filed with the Court and therefore available for the world to see as public record. Soon after the Will became public record, the daughter went on vacation. She posted all about the fun she was having at the beach on social media.

Some clever criminals had learned of her newfound inheritance through public court records. They followed her posts on social media, saw she was away from home, and took the opportunity to relieve her of her jewelry and furs while she was gone.

While this is of course an extreme story, most of us would feel safer having our affairs kept private. Trusts can accomplish this. Unlike Wills, trusts are never filed with the Court and therefore never released as public record.

Years ago, people perceived trusts as something only the wealthy would have. These days, there are many different types of trusts that even the most basic estate plan can benefit from. Trusts can be used to manage assets, personal property, insurance plans, retirement plans, real estate, and much more.

If you meet any of the following criteria, you could benefit from establishing a trust:

- Separated or recently divorced
- In a second, third or later marriage
- Not married, but in a domestic partnership
- In a same sex marriage or partnership
- Have step children
- Have a family member who requires specialized medical care
- Have foreign heirs

- Own real property
- Own foreign real estate or property in other states
- Own a business
- Have significant IRA or 401(k) assets
- Have a net worth of over $1 million

To know for certain if you could benefit from a trust, it can be helpful to meet with an experienced Georgia trusts lawyer who can assess your needs and explain the trusts most appropriate for your specific goals.

TYPES OF TRUSTS

To make our discussion of trusts a little more manageable, we have broken down this guide into the most common types of trusts. Each trust is designed to accomplish different objectives depending on your estate planning goals.

By no means is this guide a complete analysis of Georgia trusts and estate planning. It is meant to be used in conjunction with the assistance of an experienced Georgia estate planning and probate attorney.

There are many different types of trusts, but all involve a similar cast of players: (1) the person creating the trust (the "grantor"), (2) the person or corporation holding the trust (the "trustee"), and (3) the person who will benefit from the trust (the "beneficiary").

In general, a trust is a legal document that gives a trustee instructions on how to handle certain assets upon your death rather than have the Courts determine the distribution of your assets. Any assets involved in a trust will not go through probate upon your death. The grantor of the trust defines the terms of the trust and instructions for the trustee on distributions to beneficiaries.

You can create a trust while you are living ("living trust") or via a Will after your die ("testamentary trust"). Living trusts may be irrevocable or revocable. Testamentary trusts are always irrevocable.

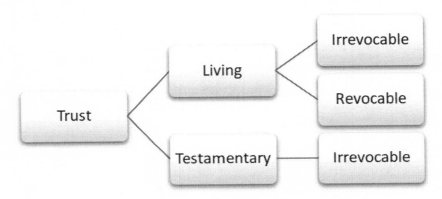

REVOCABLE TRUSTS

Also called "living trusts" or "revocable living trusts," Georgia revocable trusts (Ga. Code Ann. § 53-12-40) are perhaps the most common type of trust. These trusts are often used to accomplish what a Will would accomplish, but without the probate process and public court records. Instead of being a court-supervised distribution of assets, the assets in a revocable trust are distributed without being supervised by the Court.

Instead of your heirs receiving their inheritance months, sometimes years, down the road, the beneficiaries in a revocable trust receive their inheritance right away.

When you transfer assets into a revocable trust, you still maintain full control of the assets. As long as you are mentally competent, you can change the beneficiaries of these trusts, or add, remove or sell the assets anytime you wish.

A revocable living trust enables you to:

- Manage assets like bank accounts, businesses, homes, and investments

- Give clear instruction to how your affairs are to be managed

- Protect beneficiaries from poor decisions

- Protect beneficiaries from those looking to take advantage of them

- Have total control of the assets in your trust

- Appoint the successor who will distribute the assets to beneficiaries

Consider a couple that we helped a few years ago. We will call them "John" and "Jane." Jane explained that her mother had died a few years ago with a Last Will and Testament. It took an entire year for Jane and her siblings to receive their inheritance due to family disputes and probate delays. Now, Jane and John wanted to prepare an estate plan that would help their own children avoid those same difficulties.

Jane and John wanted their estate to pass entirely to the surviving spouse when one of them passed. Once the surviving spouse passed, they wanted everything to go immediately to their three children, divided equally. They wanted their daughter Linda to be in charge once they were both gone.

I recommended that they set up a Revocable Living Trust. They could do whatever they wanted with the trust while they were alive. They could buy, sell, manage and donate the assets – no restrictions. And nothing would change once one spouse dies. Upon the death of the surviving spouse, Linda would be named the "successor trustee," with the three children (Linda included) as equal beneficiaries of the trust upon John and Jane's deaths.

John and Jane titled their real estate into the name of the trust to avoid the probate process. They also titled their investment account into the name of John and Jane as trustees of the Revocable Living Trust. This way, upon their deaths, the investment account can be split immediately between the three children. John and Jane also titled other assets into the trust, including certificates of deposit, mineral rights and individually held stocks.

There were also assets that didn't need to be titled in the name of the trust - assets that wouldn't go through probate anyway. Non-probate assets include instruments that already have designated beneficiaries, like IRAs, 401(k)s, life insurance policies and annuities.

John died a few years later. At this point, Jane wanted to move nearer to Linda and her grandchildren. Jane's neighbor told her it would likely take a year before her house would be free to sell. But because Jane and John had set up the Revocable Living Trust, Jane was able to sell her house immediately.

Years after John's death, Jane married a man with an adult daughter. Linda and her brothers were a little worried about their inheritance. Would it go to the new husband upon Jane's death? Would it go to the step-sister?

No. According to the terms of the trust, once the second spouse dies, the assets go to the beneficiaries (John and Jane's three children). After Jane passed away, Linda was able to distribute John and Jane's $600,000 investment account immediately to herself and her two brothers, avoiding any family disputes over the money.

As you can see, a Revocable Living Trust is a wonderful alternative to a Last Will and Testament that can help ensure your loved one's avoid difficulty and delay after you have passed.

Revocable Living Trusts are also a great way to provide for blended families. For example, Georgia law does not grant step-children the same inheritance rights as natural born children and adopted children. You can make sure your step-children receive their portion of an inheritance by creating a Revocable Living Trust and naming them as beneficiaries.

Many couples feel that just having real estate under Joint Tenancy with Rights of Survivorship (JTROS) will be enough to transfer their estate to their surviving spouse upon their death. But what if John and Jane hadn't created their Revocable Living Trust, and instead had just relied on JTROS?

In this case, upon Jane's death, the real estate would go to her new husband. And upon his death, it would go to his daughter. Linda and her two brothers would have seen nothing.

What if Jane and her new husband have two children? Her new husband Fred decides to write a Will leaving his own assets to Jane, saying that if Jane dies, the estate goes to his adult daughter only (not the two new children).

Fred then passes away and Jane inherits his assets. Soon after, Jane dies, and her assets (which now include Fred's assets plus her own) pass to the two new children. Fred's original daughter gets nothing. Fred should have established a Revocable Living Trust saying that his estate would go to the surviving spouse, then after her, to his original daughter (named as beneficiary).

As you can see, Revocable Living Trusts are lifesavers for blended families. An experienced Georgia estate planning attorney can help you set up a plan that ensures your wishes are followed.

It is important to note that, because you still have control over the assets in a Revocable Trust, these assets are still vulnerable to estate taxes, creditors and lawsuit liability, and are included as assets in government benefit cut-off points. You can use other types of trusts to address these issues.

IRREVOCABLE TRUSTS

Unlike revocable trusts, in an irrevocable trust, you permanently release your interest in an asset, handing it over entirely to the trust. Because you no longer own the asset, the terms, beneficiaries and assets of irrevocable trusts cannot be changed.

But this also means the asset is safe from creditors and lawsuits. In addition, because you relinquish control of the asset, it no longer contributes to the value of your estate, thereby potentially lowering estate taxes.

Likewise, irrevocable trusts can help you protect government benefits for a special needs child by avoiding disqualification, can help avoid Medicaid spend-down provisions, and can help avoid nursing home poverty.

Assets in an irrevocable trust avoid probate and are removed from personal income tax and gift exemptions.

Testamentary Trusts

Certain types of trusts are helpful when you want to name a guardian for minor children (under age 18) and protect the inheritance you plan to leave for minor children. Many parents believe that leaving a Will and naming a guardian in that Will allows the guardian to automatically use the inheritance to care for the child. Unfortunately, this just isn't so.

First, your Will must go through probate, which as we discussed can take months to years. Second, the Court will not always appoint the guardian you name in your Will. The Court has discretion to appoint a guardian in the minor's best interest (but great consideration is given to who the parents want the guardian to be).

Once the Court appoints a guardian, the Court, not the guardian, will control the inheritance until the child reaches age 18. While the guardian will be able to use some of the inheritance, they will be heavily supervised by the Court. Once the child reaches 18, the child will receive the inheritance in a lump sum (not necessarily the best idea if you want the inheritance to provide for the child years into the future).

Additionally, the process of the Court appointing a guardian is often expensive. All expenses are paid out of the inheritance. And because the Court seeks to treat everyone equally, it may be difficult to ensure that one child receives more than another to meet any special requirements.

A better option for providing an inheritance for a minor child is through a Testamentary Trust. These trusts allow you to name a trustee who will manage the inheritance instead of the Court. You can also designate at what age the child will receive the inheritance (instead of the default age 18). Many people feel that age 21, 25 or 30 would be safer.

However, the Testamentary Trust is not perfect. These trusts can't be funded until the Will has been probated, and that takes time. Also, if you happen to become injured and unable to handle your own affairs, the trust still won't go into effect until the Will has been probated, potentially leaving your minor child without care. Finally, because the Will must be probated, your affairs become public record, which also means everyone can see what your child is inheriting.

The best option for providing an inheritance for a minor child is through a Revocable Living Trust. The Revocable Living Trust comes into existence as soon as it is signed – before you become incapacitated or pass away. This means your minor child will be cared for even if you become incapacitated.

ADVANCED TRUSTS

SPENDTHRIFT TRUSTS

A very popular trust these days, the Spendthrift Trust (Ga. Code Ann. § 53-12-80) is a clever tool for those with an adult child who may be financially irresponsible and / or possibly facing creditors.

One way to protect the inheritance of a "spendthrift" from their own spending habits and from creditors is to appoint a family member to control the release of the inheritance in small, annual distributions. However, you can imagine the potential for some serious family disputes. Most people elect to establish a Spendthrift Trust to avoid these problems, assigning an impartial third party to control the inheritance instead.

A Spendthrift Trust is basically an inheritance trust for which you hire a professional trustee to handle the distributions of the inheritance. You transfer assets into the care of an individual or corporate trustee, who delivers regular distributions to the beneficiary of the trust. The beneficiary is unable to control the trust and does not have access to the remaining funds. Meanwhile, the trust continues to generate interest and dividends.

For example, say Tom wants to leave his 40-year-old daughter Grace a $3 million inheritance. Grace is an avid (but not so talented) poker player and self-proclaimed shopaholic. Using a Spendthrift Trust, Tom establishes terms so that Grace receives just $75,000 per year from the trust.

In addition, because Grace does not own the assets contained in the trust, she is unable to use the $3 million as collateral in other dealings. If Grace fails to pay off her extensive credit card bills, creditors would not be able to touch the trust. They would only have access to her $75,000 distribution.

PET TRUSTS

Several years ago, a woman and I met for a consultation as she was concerned about what would happen to her dear Fido, Rocky and Sparky if something unexpected were to happen to her. I then realized she was referring to her pet dogs - she didn't have any children at all.

But, her concern is among the many valid concerns people have when it comes to getting their affairs in order. Approximately 65% of American households include beloved pets, and it is not uncommon for a pet to outlive its owner.

Because state law views pets as "property," we cannot name our pets as beneficiaries in a Will. So in the past, animal owners and estate planners would come up with creative ways to make sure pets had the care and support they needed after an owner's death.

For example, some people would leave their pet and a sum of money to someone they trusted in their Will. The problem with doing this is the beneficiary has no legal obligation to care for the pet.

But in 2010, the Georgia legislature enacted a law (Ga. Code Ann. § 53-12-28) that allows pet owners to create a trust for their animals, including companion animals, race horses, hunting dogs and therapy animals.

In setting up a Georgia pet trust, there are several important steps to consider.

First, ownership of the pet must be very clear since state law still considers animals to be property. The ownership of the pet must be pre-determined. Microchipping your pet with your name and address, keeping tags on your pet and other precautions can help prove ownership if a pet becomes lost. Providing photocopies of your trust to everyone involved can help ensure ownership of the pet is clear.

Second, your pet trust must name a "guardian" (the person or organization who will be taking care of your pet) and a "trustee" (the person or organization that will handle the trust's finances). The guardian and trustee can be the same person or organization, but I don't always recommend it. Since the trustee oversees the guardian's care of the pet, having a separate trustee can ensure the guardian is following your care instructions. You will also want to select a successor guardian and successor trustee should the original individuals be unable to perform their roles.

Third, your pet trust must be properly funded. Otherwise, the guardian may not have the proper incentive to care for your pet the way you wish. Make sure to consider your pet's age (they are more expensive with age), the type of pet (race horses require more care than the average dog), and any special care needs. You can specify every aspect of your pet's care, including the brand of food it eats, how much food to feed, your chosen veterinarian and more.

And finally, you will need to name remainder beneficiaries. While the pet is the primary beneficiary of the trust, remainder beneficiaries will receive whatever is left over once the pet dies. Typically, owners will name a charity or animal hospital as a remainder beneficiary, but you could also name a family member.

MEDICAID IRREVOCABLE TRUSTS

A Medicaid Irrevocable Trust is primarily designed to prevent nursing home poverty. Most Americans will spend at least some time in an assisted living facility, nursing home or receive some form of home health care. And this can get expensive. It costs an average of $65,000 per year to live in a Georgia nursing home – double that if you want to live in the home as a couple.

So most people use Georgia Medicaid to help pay for these services. In fact, around three out of four Georgia nursing home residents pay for their facility services using Medicaid. But you have to be eligible to receive those benefits.

One requirement to qualify for Georgia Medicaid is that your annual income must be less than $2,250 per month and you must have less than $2,000 in assets. In Georgia, your home (valued at less than $560,000), personal belongings and one vehicle may be exempt from this resource limit, but many people still have more than $2,000 in assets after subtracting their home and vehicle.

Some couples end up having to sell their assets to qualify for their nursing home care. But you can avoid this need to "spend-down" assets by setting up a Medicaid Irrevocable Trust. These types of trusts protect your non-exempt assets while still allowing you to be eligible for Medicaid coverage of long-term care expenses.

While you could gift your non-exempt assets, its best to transfer your non-exempt assets into a Medicaid Irrevocable Trust and let your children inherit them instead. This helps them to avoid capital gains tax and you still get to keep some degree of control over your assets during your lifetime.

ASSET PROTECTION TRUSTS

Many of our clients work in an industry susceptible to lawsuits. Since its illegal to transfer assets to avoid creditor judgments, smart estate planners will protect their assets before a lawsuit ever happens.

We are all at risk of losing our assets to a lawsuit. If you come across hard times and default on loans, creditors will come after everything you own. If the neighbor is seriously injured on your property, you might have to pay their lost wages and a lifetime of medical expenses. Many folks lose their hard-earned property to divorce.

But certain professions are at even higher risk for lawsuits. Business owners face EEOC lawsuits, workplace injury lawsuits, sexual harassment lawsuits, trademark infringement lawsuits, and breach of contract claims. Physicians and lawyers face malpractice lawsuits.

Persons involved in high-risk business ventures or who work in high-risk professions like the medical or legal fields should take steps to shield themselves from the liabilities that come with those fields.

Many states require or suggest that professionals such as doctors, lawyers, accountants, architects, dentists, land surveyors, veterinarians, even harbor pilots, become incorporated as a certain business entity. Rather than a sole proprietorship, it is safest to incorporate or function under a Limited Liability Company (LLC) or Professional Limited Liability Company (PLLC).

Asset Protection Trusts can also be used to protect your assets from lawsuits and liability. By transferring assets into an irrevocable trust, you are no longer in control of those assets. They are no longer part of your estate and therefore are not accessible to judgment creditors.

Currently, several states (around 15) provide protection for self-settled Domestic Asset Protection Trusts (DAPT). The DAPT is a trust created within the United States (hence "domestic") for the purpose of asset protection. Unfortunately, Georgia does not currently protect DAPTs. But an experienced Georgia estate planning lawyer can help you develop other options for setting up a successful Asset Protection Trust.

Overseas Asset Protection Trusts are another way to use the law to protect your assets so that your children and grandchildren can benefit from your hard work. You may also want to consider a Foreign Asset Protection Trust – placing your assets in a jurisdiction that the U.S. courts cannot enforce judgment against.

In addition, any revocable trusts you own will become irrevocable upon your death, protecting them from judgment creditors and liability.

Setting up a Georgia Asset Protection Trust can be a complex process that is best accomplished with the aid of an expert. If you are a business owner, physician, lawyer or other high-risk industry professional, we recommend that you meet with an experienced Georgia estate planning lawyer who can evaluate your assets and determine the best strategy for protecting your estate from potential lawsuits and liability.

CHILDREN'S INHERITANCE TRUSTS

Do you have an over-controlling daughter-in-law? Maybe a not-quite-perfect son-in-law? Believe me, you aren't alone. Many folks come into The Farrell Law Firm concerned about making their inheritance divorce proof. They want to make sure that the family business, family heirlooms or other special assets stay within the family.

Prenuptial agreements can help to protect your child's inheritance from their spouse by listing the inheritance as outside of the martial property and describing how the inheritance is to be divided upon divorce.

However, a Children's Inheritance Trust is often a more efficient option for those seeking to protect their child's inheritance from divorce or creditors. These trusts can reduce or even eliminate estate taxes, last for the beneficiary's entire lifetime, and pass to the beneficiary's children upon their death.

A Children's Inheritance Trust segregates the assets meant for your child from those that your child and their spouse have accumulated (marital property), so the inheritance is not subject to division in divorce. This type of trust can be either revocable or irrevocable.

In a revocable Children's Inheritance Trust, you control the assets during your lifetime, but these assets are still vulnerable to creditors of your own. In an Irrevocable Children's Inheritance Trust, you relinquish control of the assets, but they are safe from any creditors or judgements against you, the grantor.

Be sure to select an independent trustee, such as a trust company or bank, for your Children's Inheritance Trust, as it can be difficult for your child to have to stand up to their spouse in financial dealings. In disputes, friends or family are more likely to give into a family member's demands for money rather than protect the inheritance.

2503(C) MINOR'S TRUSTS

As opposed to a Children's Inheritance Trust that is meant for an adult child, a Minor's Trust sets aside an inheritance for a beneficiary under the age of 18. Minor's Trusts effectively protect the inheritance by assigning a trustee who will have some discretion in distributing the funds for the health, education, maintenance and support (HEMS) of the minor. In the event of your death, the minor only receives distributions and cannot access the entire funds until he or she reaches a designated age (21). When the minor reaches that designated age, the property and any generated income can be transferred to the beneficiary in full.

A 2503(c) Minor's Trust is designed to avoid gift taxes. Gifts valued at $15,000 or less (per year per recipient) are generally exempt from federal gift taxes, as long as the gift is received. But Minor's Trusts don't deliver the asset to the minor outright, so are not exempt from gift taxes.

However, IRS Code §2053(c) offers an exception to this rule. It allows the $15,000 exemption to apply to Minor's Trust assets as long as:

1. The minor is the sole primary beneficiary of the trust,
2. A trustee has discretion on income and principal distributions
3. The beneficiary receives all trust assets and generated income at age 21.
4. If the beneficiary dies before age 21, the entire trust is made payable to the beneficiary's estate.

There are adaptations to Minor's Trusts that allow you to avoid gift taxes while keeping the inheritance from the beneficiary until a later age than 21. Consult with an experienced Georgia estate planning attorney to learn more about these Minor's Trust modifications.

In addition, the grantor of a Minor's Trust can exclude those assets from their estate for purposes of estate taxes (as long as the grantor is not the trustee). And there are no restrictions on the assets you can transfer to a 2053(c) Minor's Trust (as opposed to the restrictions on Uniform Transfers to Minors (UTMA) accounts).

SUPPLEMENTAL NEEDS TRUSTS

Many people come into our office with concerns about a special needs child. If you need help supplementing the needs of that person, or if that person receives government benefits for their special needs, we will set up what we call a Supplemental Needs Trust.

A Supplemental Needs Trust is a type of Special Needs Trust designed to provide benefits and protect assets for individuals with physical or mental disabilities, without critically separating or affecting their qualifications for government health care benefits that they receive, including long-term nursing care Medicaid benefits.

Supplemental Needs Trusts can also be used to receive an inheritance or settlement proceeds on behalf of a special needs person, in order to safeguard their Medicaid eligibility.

In Supplemental Needs Trusts, the trustee holds legal title to the assets for the beneficiary. A Supplemental Needs Trust remains valid as long as the trust meets several requirements (42 US Code §1396p(d)(4)(A)):

- It is an Irrevocable Spendthrift Trust
- Beneficiary is significantly impaired
- It is established before the beneficiary reaches age 65
- It functions under a separate employer identification number
- It includes requisite Medicaid payback provisions

Supplemental Needs Trusts only allow the trustee to pay for needs that the government will not cover. They aren't designed to provide the beneficiary with support and maintenance and don't offer regular fund distributions.

In most cases, Medicaid can disallow asset transfers any time they find that the transfers are made specifically to qualify for

Medicaid. But a disabled beneficiary can supply their own assets for a Supplemental Needs Trust (first-party, self-settled).

For first party, self-settled Supplemental Needs Trusts, the Medicaid payback provision is required. This provision says that any assets in a Supplemental Needs Trust are subject to a Medicaid lien upon the beneficiary's death. The provision does not apply to Supplemental Needs Trusts established by individuals other than the beneficiary (third-party trusts).

SPECIAL NEEDS TRUSTS

What about special needs individuals who don't receive any government assistance? For these cases, we also offer what we call Special Needs Trusts. As opposed to Supplemental Needs Trusts, Special Needs Trusts are designed to accommodate the specific needs of a person regardless of any type of government assistance they might receive.

In a Special Needs Trust, you designate a trustee to take care of the beneficiary in the instance that you are not able. These trusts are valuable for those who have concerns that the beneficiary may not be capable to handle themselves financially. Special Needs Trusts can protect the inheritance or assets of someone with special needs. In addition, these trusts can also help a special needs individual maintain their eligibility for government benefits.

Like Supplemental Needs Trusts, Special Needs Trusts include both first-party, self-settled trusts and traditional third-party trusts and may require Medicaid payback provisions in first-party trusts.

As you can see, there are many different types of trusts. Those listed above are among the most common. A wide variety of trusts and combinations of trusts are available to meet every individual's specific needs. Your best bet for deciding which trusts can maximize your estate plan is to sit down with an experienced Georgia estate planning attorney, discuss your goals, and design a plan customized to your life.

PROCESS OF SETTING UP A TRUST

Establishing your trust can be a short process or a fairly complex one depending on your assets, the number of beneficiaries, and other factors. You will want to make sure you take the time to thoughtfully consider what the best thing is for you and your loved ones. A Georgia estate planning lawyer can help guide you through the process of setting up your trust.

Setting up your trust will include several steps:

- Selecting the trust that is right for you

- Writing and preparing the trust document

- Naming your beneficiaries and trustees

- Signing the document in the presence of a notary

- Funding the trust and transferring ownership of property to the name of the trust

Don't Forget to Keep Track of Your Trust Assets

One of the major complaints that family member's have following a loved one's passing is that it took them forever to figure out what mom or dad had. Some even have to wait by the mailbox for all of the bills to come through before they can make a final determination about the family's assets.

To make it easier on the family, you should keep track and provide proof of every asset you have or that has been transferred to your trust. Keep this list with your other estate planning documents and review this list annually to make sure nothing has been transferred in or out that is not on the list.

As a general rule, The Farrell Law Firm provides a section in the Portfolio for you to make such an inventory.

Here are some things you will want to include on your list:

- **Bank accounts:** List all bank accounts - checking, savings or otherwise – plus bank locations and account numbers.

- **Beneficiary designations:** List all insurance policies and other assets that have beneficiary designations (and who those beneficiary designations are). If you have stock certificates, be sure to include a photocopy of those with your estate planning documents.

- **Debts:** Include a list of any credit card or other debts you may have.

- **Document locations**: Keep a list noting the location of any important documents, including your original Will and Self-Proving Affidavit.

- **Investments:** Be sure to include any investment accounts in this list.

- **Real estate:** The legal description is very handy to have, but if you transferred the real estate to the trust, then the deed doing so should be kept with the list. If you don't have a copy of the deed to the property to include with the list, definitely include the address of the property. This goes for real estate in your state of residence, another state or another country.

- **Vehicles:** List any vehicles you may own. Included with this list, keep copies of any titles to your vehicles, or the original title if you happen to own the vehicle free and clear.

Additionally, there are other estate planning vehicles you can use to make it easy on your family when you're no longer here. An experienced Georgia estate planning attorney can help tailor your estate plan to meet your specific needs.

Living Trust Administration Process

As you can probably guess, the trust administration process is usually much simpler, faster and less costly when compared to the probate process. No court or lawyers need be involved.

When the grantor of the trust passes away, the trustee will take measures to make sure the grantor's wishes are carried out. The trust agreement typically provides the trustee with instructions on their role in distributing the trust assets, how and when the assets are to be distributed, and to whom the assets will go.

The trustee may be required to transfer trust asset ownership to beneficiaries, take care of transfer taxes, change property deeds or titles, and file taxes for the trust.

Once the trust administration process is complete, the beneficiaries become the legal owners of the assets they receive.

ADVANCED ESTATE PLANNING

We refer to the material in this section as "advanced estate planning," not because you need advanced knowledge of estate planning to understand it, but because it covers specific types of estates that involve a more complex estate plan.

In this section, we introduce a variety of estate planning strategies that can help maximize your estate by minimizing estate and gift taxes and protecting your assets from liability. The estate planning tactics offered in this guide are especially helpful for high- and ultra-high net worth families, high-liability professions, and business owners.

TAX MITIGATION TOOLS FOR HIGH-NET WORTH FAMILIES

Estate planning for households with assets of $10 million plus can present some significant challenges, and a lack of solid estate planning can mean devastating losses for you and future generations.

94

Even with some level of estate planning in place, studies show that 70% of high net worth family assets won't last beyond the third generation. Some loss of fortune may be attributed to financial carelessness or bad investments, but much of it is lost to estate taxes.

Up to 50% or more of your net-worth can be lost to estate taxes per generation.

Those high net worth families whose fortunes hold up for six generations and beyond often have a team of financial and estate planning specialists who know how to generate a plan that takes the amount lost to taxes to the absolute minimum.

An understanding of how high net worth families successfully minimize tax burdens can help you work with your estate planning team to make smart decisions for your family's future.

Federal Estate and Gift Taxes 101

In order to minimize taxes, it is critical that you first understand what access the government has to your estate. For Georgia residents, this includes federal estate and gift taxes. The federal government charges estate taxes to transfer your property when you die. Federal estate taxes use the fair market value of your assets (cash, real estate, securities, insurance, annuities, trusts, business interests, etc.) at the time of your death – minus certain deductions.

As of January 2018, estates with assets and prior taxable gifts exceeding $11,200,000 must file federal estate taxes. And this exemption is generous. In 2017 and prior, the exemption has been $5.6 million (note that the current $11.2 million exemption is set to revert back to $5.6 million on January 1, 2026).

Currently, an individual could transfer up to $11.2 million in assets during their life or at death and avoid federal estate and gift taxes. Anything over $11.2 million ($22.4 million for married couples filing jointly) may be taxed up to 40%. Federal estate taxes must be paid within nine months of death. If no cash is available, your heirs or beneficiaries will have to liquidate assets to pay.

In addition, some states require a state estate tax, meaning the estate could be taxed a total of 50% or more. As of July 1, 2014, Georgia has eliminated state estate taxes.

High net worth individuals and families will also want to take advantage of the annual gift tax exclusion that allows tax-free asset transfers of up to $15,000 per year ($30,000 per beneficiary for married couples filing jointly).

Maximizing estate tax exclusions and controlling gift taxes is key to preserving your fortune for generations. There are several ways high net worth households can accomplish this. A clever combination of any number of these tactics works best.

Maximize Estate Tax Exemptions

Obviously, you will want to maximize your estate tax exemptions. Affluent Georgia households who can avoid estate taxes may be able to provide support for an additional two generations.

In 2013, Congress permanently passed the law of portability, allowing a surviving spouse to use both their own estate tax exemption and the deceased spouse's unused exemption, as long as estate tax returns are filed promptly after the first spouse's death.

So when the first spouse dies, they can leave all their assets to the surviving spouse. Because of unlimited marital deductions, the government won't tax the surviving spouse when they first spouse dies. Then, upon the second spouse's death, portability allows the entire estate to pass tax-free to heirs and beneficiaries upon the second spouse's death – as long as the couple's estate is under $22.4 million (though any asset appreciation will be taxed).

But what about married couples with estates that exceed $22.4 million? These households can still preserve the first spouse's estate tax exemption by establishing a tax-advantage trust containing the first spouse's assets. The surviving spouse can access these assets, and even act as trustee, but the contained assets AND any appreciation (until the second spouse's death) aren't included in the taxable estate (even if the appreciation is over the exemption amount).

With a tax-advantage trust, you can avoid taxation on appreciation, you can avoid estate taxes on estates over $22.4 million, and it can even help you avoid estate taxes when the exemption drops back down to $5.6 million ($11.2 million for married couples) in 2026.

Of course, you could include a similar tax-planning provision in your Will, but your beneficiaries would then have to go through probate expenses and wait months to years for access to their inheritance.

Purchase Life Insurance

Life insurance policies are another good way to pass wealth to your loved ones or to charities you care about. If you buy your life insurance policy at the right time, it can effectively replace any estate taxes or gifted assets.

But upon your death, the proceeds from your life insurance policy are included in your estate value. To avoid paying estate taxes on your policy, it is best to set up an Irrevocable Life Insurance Trust (ILIT). With an ILIT, you can name a trustee and have that trustee purchase the life insurance policy on your behalf. This eliminates the policy proceeds from your taxable estate.

You can even name the ILIT as a beneficiary and set it up to distribute portions of the trust to family members for years to come, keeping the bulk of the trust safe from overspending or creditors. Note that for an ILIT to work, you have to survive at least three-years after initiating the trust.

Reduce Your Estate

Because estate taxes apply only to those assets you own directly, transferring ownership of your assets outside of your estate can reduce estate taxes significantly. You can do this using:

- Family Incorporation
- Charitable Trusts
- IRA Qualified Charitable Donations (QCD)
- Generation Skipping Trusts
- Tax-Free Gifts
- Buildup Equity Retirement Trusts
- Qualified Personal Residence Trusts (QPRT)
- Grantor Retained Trusts
- Intentionally Defective Grantor Trusts (IDGT)

Family Incorporation

Setting up a Family Limited Partnership (FLP) or Family Limited Liability Company (FLLC) can help reduce estate taxes. In an FLP, family members pool money to operate a business. They serve as general and limited partners and can buy shares of the business and profit from those shares. FLLCs are similar to FLPs except they are a corporate entity for which family members may act as managers.

You transfer assets into the FLP or FLLC, act as general partner or manager, and collect ownership interest. Typically, older family members will gift limited partner interest to younger family members, thereby reducing estate tax.

Charitable Trusts

Charitable trusts allow you to reduce estate taxes while benefiting any charities you are passionate about. Charitable trusts are very popular, and a number of variations are available.

Charitable Remainder Trusts (CRT) can reduce your income and estate taxes by transferring income-producing assets into an irrevocable trust and taking advantage of charitable income tax deductions. Upon your death, the assets go to the charity of your choice. During your life, the trust reinvests in income-producing assets, you collect ongoing income, the assets sell at market value, and no capital gains tax applies – meaning you often collect more than you would selling the asset yourself.

Charitable Remainder Annuity Trusts (CRAT) transfer assets into a trust that pays a fixed amount each year until the grantor's death, when they go to the designated charity. Charitable Remainder Unitrusts (CRUT) distribute a fixed percentage of assets to a beneficiary over a fixed term, after which the assets go to the charity.

As opposed to CRTs, Charitable Lead Trusts (CLT) are also a great way to reduce estate taxes but don't pay income to the grantor. Instead, the income goes to the charity for a fixed term or until your death, after which the assets go to your heirs or beneficiaries.

Charitable Lead Annuity Trusts (CLAT) give a part of the income interest to a charitable organization and another part of the interest to the grantor or a beneficiary. Charitable Lead Unitrusts (CLUT) allow the grantor to give a variable annual amount of the trust to a charity for a certain number of years. After the term ends, trust assets go to the grantor or a beneficiary.

"Shark Fin" Charitable Lead Annuity Trusts transfer small payments into a CLAT for a few years, then transfer a large lump sum payment into the CLAT toward the end of the term (creating a "shark fin" shaped curve of payments). By increasing the amount paid to charity over time, assets in the trust have more time to grow.

IRA Qualified Charitable Donations (QCD)

If you are at least 70.5 years old and own an IRA, you can donate a certain amount ($100,000 per individual) of your IRA each year directly to a non-profit organization to reduce the size of your estate.

Generation Skipping Trusts

If you are concerned about your child's inheritance adding to the value of the estate, you can set up a Generation Skipping Trust. This type of trust avoids generation-skipping taxes by transferring assets directly to your grandchildren, bypassing your children.

The Generation Skipping Trust transfers assets to any beneficiary other than a spouse or ex-spouse who is at least 37.5 years younger than the grantor. Generation-skipping trusts can still benefit the grantor's children since they are able to access any income generated by the trust's assets.

Tax-Free Gifts

Transferring gifts out of your estate before you pass (preferably appreciating gifts) is one way to reduce estate taxes. The recipient will have to pay capital gains tax when they sell the gift and at cost basis. But, the capital gains tax could be less than what the estate tax would be if you held onto the asset.

Gifts to charities, and educational and medical institutions are always tax-free. You can also give up to $15,000 in tax-free gifts each year per beneficiary. If you have three kids and six grandchildren, you could give them each $15,000 and reduce your estate by $135,000 per year.

Buildup Equity Retirement Trusts

Under Internal Revenue Code §2056, an individual can transfer an unlimited amount of assets to their spouse at any time (during life or death), tax free. The problem with this is that any asset transferred to a surviving spouse (plus appreciation) can be included in the spouse's taxable estate.

Instead of using the unlimited marital deduction, you can set up a Buildup Equity Retirement Trust and use the annual gift tax exclusion to grant gifts to your spouse – eliminating the gift assets from gift and estate taxes.

Also known as a Spousal Limited Access Trust (SLAT), the grantor creates this trust to transfer assets from their estate into a trust that benefits their spouse. The grantor's spouse has indirect access to the trust, and assets are excluded from the taxable estates of both spouses. When the grantor's spouse dies, the assets pass to designated beneficiaries without incurring gift or estate taxes.

You can grow earnings tax free as long as you draft the trust so the grantor pays income taxes. In this trust, remember to limit your annual gifts to $5,000 or 5% of trust balance up to the annual gift tax exclusion to avoid estate and gift tax.

Qualified Personal Residence Trusts (QPRT)

You can eliminate your residence from your estate value and reduce its value as a gift with a QPRT. Transferring the house to the trust over a term of several years means you can remain in the home with retained interest until the end of the trust, when ownership transfers to your beneficiaries as remainder interest (at which point you could arrange to still live there).

Because the owner retains part of the property's value, the gift value is less than the fair market value, and so is incurred gift tax.

Of course, the longer the term, the smaller the remainder interest given to beneficiaries and lower the gift tax. But keep in mind that if the grantor passes away before the term is up, the assets go back into the grantor's estate.

Grantor Retained Trusts

Similar to QPRTs, you can avoid estate and gift taxes by setting up irrevocable Grantor Retained Annuity Trusts (GRAT) and Grantor Retained Unitrusts (GRUT) to transfer income-producing assets into the trust over several years.

While the assets are no longer included in your estate, you still collect the income. These trusts also reduce the value of the gift for your beneficiaries. What the assets produce will pass to your beneficiaries estate tax-free.

- GRAT: Grantor collects an annual payment for a fixed term, after which the remaining assets are gifted to the beneficiary
- GRUT: Grantor collects a fluctuating income for a fixed term (or for the grantor's lifetime).

Intentionally Defective Grantor Trusts (IDGT)

Intentionally Defective Grantor Trusts (IDGT) are irrevocable trusts that allow you to reduce the value of your estate by freezing certain assets while continuing to pay income taxes.

All of these strategies can help high net worth individuals and families expand their fortunes across numerous generations. Our Farrell Law Firm attorney and staff have developed an arsenal of successful programs that can minimize your tax liability and help ensure that your legacy lives on for generations to come.

PROFESSIONALS

ASSET PROTECTION PLANS FOR HIGH-RISK PROFESSIONALS

W e are all at risk of losing our assets to a lawsuit. If you come across hard times and default on loans, creditors will come after everything you own. If the neighbor is seriously injured on your property, you might have to pay their lost wages and a lifetime of medical expenses. Many folks lose their hard-earned property to divorce.

But some individuals work in industries that are particularly susceptible to liability. Most people know that doctors and lawyers are at high risk for malpractice lawsuits, but other professionals are also considered at high risk for liability, including:

- Contractors

- Educators

- Finance professionals

- Food industry professionals

- Realtors

- IT professionals

- Therapists

These hard-working professionals must shield their estates from judgment creditors if they want to provide for their loved ones for generations. Proper estate planning is a must for people who work in high-risk professions, and asset protection is key.

There are a couple of things to remember about protecting your assets from liability. First, you must understand the concept of fraudulent conveyance. Because state and federal laws void asset transfers that attempt to avoid debt, high-risk professionals must act preemptively and transfer their assets well before any lawsuit arises.

A claim is considered reasonably foreseeable when you "knew or should have known" that a claim was likely to arise. Once a claim is foreseeable, it is usually too late to defend your assets from creditors by transferring them out of your estate. Smart estate planners will protect their assets before a lawsuit ever happens.

Second, the more control you have over your assets, the lower the level of protection. You don't want to give up control of all of your assets, but you don't want a large portion of your estate to fall victim to a multi-million dollar suit. An experienced Georgia estate planning attorney will be able to help you establish a balance that will achieve your goals.

Several strategies for asset protection are available to high-risk professionals, including:

- Liability insurance

- Incorporation

- Exempt instruments

- Irrevocable trusts

- Self-settled trusts

Liability Insurance

Liability insurance is the first step in protecting your assets, and many medical, legal and financial professions require it. Liability insurance allows you to maintain control over your assets, but protection is limited to the policy amount. Depending on the industry, settlements and verdicts can easily surpass policy limits. It is at this point that your estate assets become vulnerable.

Incorporation

Another level of protection involves creating and maintaining proper business entities. One of the more popular business forms for liability protection is the Limited Liability Company (LLC). The LLC allows for limited liability for the members or owners. Additionally, the requirements to maintain the corporate status aren't as rigid as with a normal corporation. The better protection from liability and the easier to maintain corporate formalities makes the LLC a go-to business model for asset protection.

In fact, many states require or suggest that professionals such as doctors, lawyers, accountants, architects, dentists, land surveyors, veterinarians, even harbor pilots, become incorporated as a certain business entity. Rather than a sole proprietorship, it is safest to incorporate or function under a LLC, Professional Limited Liability Company (PLLC) or Professional Corporation (PC).

As a high-risk professional, you would invest in the PLLC and get a limited partnership or non-voting membership interest. You would name an irrevocable trust as general partner or voting member. Creditors may attempt to get a charging order, but your limitations on asset control and related tax liabilities are particularly unappealing to creditors.

If you are a professional and you need to incorporate, I can't stress the importance enough of retaining a Georgia business or estate planning attorney to help you. Creating, keeping, and maintaining proper corporate formalities is key to obtaining limited liability from potential loss of assets.

Exempt Instruments

Another basic level of protection involves taking advantage of whatever exemptions you can. Certain assets are exempt from creditors if created prior to any claim against you. Under the Employee Retirement Income Security Act (ERISA) and Georgia state law, assets held in IRAs and 401(k)s are exempt from creditors, as long as the assets remain in the fund.

Cash Balance Pension Plans are also a good choice. Under ERISA, cash balance pension plans are safe from creditors. But these plans can be expensive. As part of the plan, your practice must make employee contributions, so these plans work best for smaller practices.

The bottom line is, certain financial instruments may be protected by either state or federal law. A qualified Georgia estate planning attorney can help you discover where you are protected and where you are open to liability.

Irrevocable Trusts

Asset protection trusts can also be used to safeguard your assets from lawsuits and liability. By transferring assets into the name of an irrevocable trust, you are no longer in control of those assets. They are no longer part of your estate and therefore are not accessible to judgment creditors.

Although asset protection trusts are irrevocable, they still offer some degree of control and a great many benefits. As the grantor, you establish the terms of the trust and exactly how your assets are to be maintained and distributed. Because you relinquish control of the asset, it no longer contributes to the value of your estate, thereby potentially lowering estate taxes.

Asset protection trusts can help you protect government benefits for a special needs child by avoiding disqualification, can help avoid Medicaid spend-down provisions, and can help avoid nursing home poverty. Assets in an irrevocable trust avoid probate and are removed from personal income tax and gift exemptions.

Self-Settled Trusts

A higher level of protection involves self-settled trusts, which are irrevocable trusts you are able to fund with your own assets and name yourself as a beneficiary. Because of jurisdiction conflicts and/or state law, the trust's assets are shielded from creditors. Because you can name yourself as beneficiary, you retain significant access to your assets.

One popular self-settled trust is the Domestic Asset Protection Trust, or DAPT. Currently, several states (around 15) provide protection for self-settled Domestic Asset Protection Trusts (DAPT). Unfortunately, Georgia does not currently protect DAPTs.

Offshore or Foreign Asset Protection Trusts are a great option for Georgia professionals seeking to protect assets from liability. Offshore asset protection trusts are established in a non-U.S. jurisdiction, keeping your assets out of the reach of creditors. Since both U.S. and foreign laws are involved in establishing foreign trusts, it is important to obtain the advice of an experienced Georgia estate planning attorney when planning this type of self-settled trust.

Setting up an estate plan that successfully protects your assets from judgment creditors can be a complex process that is best accomplished with the aid of an expert. If you are a physician, lawyer or other high-risk industry professional, we recommend that you meet with an experienced Georgia estate planning lawyer who can evaluate your assets and determine the best strategy for protecting your estate from potential lawsuits and liability.

ESTATE PLANNING STRATEGIES FOR BUSINESS OWNERS

Like high-risk professionals, business owners must protect themselves from some degree of liability risk due to EEOC lawsuits, workplace injury lawsuits, sexual harassment lawsuits, trademark infringement lawsuits, and breach of contract claims.

Of equal importance, all types of business owners (partnerships, corporations, limited liability partnerships (LLP), LLCs or PCs) must take action to protect their business in the event of their incapacitation or death.

Careful estate planning can help you to preserve your business and ensure a future source of income for your loved ones. There are several estate planning strategies that business owners can benefit from, including:

- Business succession planning
- Buy-sell agreements
- Charitable remainder trusts
- Lack of control and lack of marketability discounts
- Partnerships and incorporation
- Grantor retained trusts
- IRS §6166 deferral / §303 redemption
- Irrevocable Life Insurance Trust (ILIT)
- Estate and gift tax deductions / exclusions

Business Succession Planning

Business succession planning is something every business owner should take time out to do. Assign management and ownership successors ahead of time. Set up any necessary training. Draft any corporate restructuring to facilitate business interest transfers into trusts for heirs and beneficiaries.

Many business owners choose to name a business executor in their Last Will and Testament. You can also designate a power of attorney to handle the business' legal and financial affairs if you are no longer able. An experienced Georgia estate planning attorney can help make sure your succession plan covers all bases.

Buy-Sell Agreements

All business owners can benefit from a buy-sell agreement between owners. These agreements allow you to plan the transfer of your ownership interests to your loved ones should you choose to leave the business, or upon your incapacitation or death. They cover business management, terms of payment, your preferred transfer procedures and how business interests will be valued and priced.

Preset prices help prevent disputes between others in the event that you leave the business. These agreements also help the business avoid IRS §170 bargain sales. If you're worried about losing your business interests in a divorce, buy-sell agreements can also restrict interest transfers to those involved in the business. You can draft this agreement at any time and amend it at any time.

Charitable Remainder Trusts

Transferring your business shares into a CRT is a great method for lowering the estate taxes imposed on your beneficiaries while benefitting your favorite non-profit organization. Upon your death, a CRT will donate your business shares to your chosen organization.

Lack of Control and Lack of Marketability Discounts

By gifting partial business interests to family members before your death, rather than after, you may be able to reduce estate and gift taxes. Certain business owners who gift partial interests to loved ones can take advantage of minority (lack of control) discounts and discounts on lack of marketability (DLOM). Both of these discounts reduce the value of the gift, lowering the gift tax and potentially qualifying it for the annual gift tax exemption.

Minority discounts reduce the value when the ownership of a business interest is worth less than the equity value (the minority interest doesn't control critical business aspects). Conversely, DLOMs reduce the value when selling the interest to a third-party would prove challenging.

Partnerships and Incorporation

Family Limited Partnerships (FLP) are also solid estate planning tools for business owners. Basically, you transfer interests into an FLP made of a general partner and limited partners. You control or own the general partner (LLC or corporation), who owns 1% of the business. Limited partnership interests make up the remaining 99% of the business. The general partner manages income flow to limited partners and safeguards family members from liability.

These partnerships allow you to gift business interests to family members with gift tax discounts (using DLOM and minority discounts of up to 40%). The FLP also protects limited partnership interests from creditors since the general partner restricts transfer of interests.

In addition, business owners could put real estate in a Limited Liability Company (LLC). Like FLPs, you can take advantage of DLOM and minority discounts when gifting this property to loved ones.

Grantor Retained Trusts

Owners of businesses (other than S corporations) can avoid estate and gift taxes by setting up irrevocable GRATs. You transfer business interests into the trust and collect income over a fixed number of years. At the end of the fixed term, the business interests go to designated beneficiaries.

Gifting business interests through a GRAT reduces the gift's value for tax purposes. Any appreciation that accumulates after transfer into the trust also avoids estate and gift taxes at the end of the term (if the grantor is still alive).

IRS §6166 Deferral / §303 Redemption

Under Internal Revenue Code §6166, if your business interest is more than 35% of your gross estate and remains in the family, your family may be able to defer estate taxes for up to 14 years after your death (rather than the usual 9 months after death), giving your loved ones more time to pay estate taxes and potentially protecting your business. Note that the IRS charges interest during this deferral period.

Under Internal Revenue Code §303, if your business interest is more than 35% of your gross estate and remains in the family, your family may be able to use your stock to pay estate taxes without income tax liability. This may not be an available option if your business lacks capital surplus.

Irrevocable Life Insurance Trust (ILIT)

ILITs are another great way for certain business owners to protect their assets from estate taxes. Upon your death, the trustee uses your life insurance policy proceeds to pay any estate taxes related to your business interest.

If you use the IRS §6166 deferral, you can invest the life insurance over the deferral years to help pay estate taxes and incurred IRS interest. If you use the IRS §303 redemption, your life insurance proceeds can help pay estate taxes when your capital surplus is low.

Estate and Gift Tax Deductions / Exclusions

Business owners can also take advantage of several estate and gift tax deductions and exclusions. Of course, there is the annual gift tax exclusion, allowing the business owner to gift up to $15,000 in business interests each year per recipient.

In addition to this, business owners can use all or part of their lifetime gift tax exclusion at any time. This exclusion allows you to gift a certain amount in assets to family members without incurring estate or gift tax. As of 2018, individuals can gift up to $11.2 million tax-free over their lifetime (or leave up to $11.2 million as a tax-free gift after death).

Finally, married business owners can use the marital deduction to transfer an unlimited value of assets to their spouse without incurring estate or gift tax as long as the transfers are outright or placed in a marital trust.

A combination of several of these options can ensure that your loved ones avoid the adversities associated with a business that is ill-prepared for your absence. An experienced Georgia estate planning lawyer can help you create a detailed succession plan and minimize taxes – both key to ensuring your wishes are fulfilled and your family is taken care of.

DO I NEED AN ESTATE PLANNING LAWYER?

You can't browse the internet or watch television without seeing an advertisement for "Draft your own Will online" and Do-It-Yourself Will-writing software packages. Of course, we all want what's easiest, fastest and cheapest.

But most of us aren't willing to sacrifice effectiveness, especially when it comes to planning for our loved ones' future.

While DIY estate planning is certainly possible, there are risks involved with crafting an estate plan alone. After testing several common Will-writing products, Consumer Reports found that all are inadequate unless the simplest of estate plans is all you require (meaning no children, no second or third marriages, no trusts, and no concerns about cutting costs, optimizing taxes or avoiding probate).

Unlike most Americans, professional estate planning and probate attorneys have spent decades perfecting the art of the perfect estate plan. DIY wills are therefore much more susceptible to error without assistance from an estate lawyer. Without a lawyer, you run the risk that your power of attorney, will or trust won't function as planned or isn't legally valid at all.

For example, state law governs how an estate plan must be prepared to be legal. There are hundreds of minute details that only an experienced estate planning and probate attorney will be aware of. State law decides which forms must be filed with the court, and under what conditions signatures may be deemed legally valid. Georgia law also lays out numerous restrictions on who can be an executor, financial power of attorney, medical power of attorney, trustee, witness to a trust or witness to a will.

On top of that, state law changes regularly and documents must be updated to comply with these changes. An estate lawyer is aware of any changes in state laws that may affect your plan and knows how to quickly change your documents to keep things compliant.

Mistakes could cost your family thousands of dollars to repair. Without an estate lawyer to help prepare your documents, probate lawyers, the IRS or the Georgia Department of Revenue could steal away with a majority of your family's inheritance.

Trust Mills

I want to take a moment to warn you about "Trust Mills." These are companies, always non-lawyers, who are self-described estate planning experts that don't really give you any advice at all, but steer you towards the most expensive plan they can get away with. They can't give you legal advice because they are not lawyers.

Interestingly, I'm aware of one that promotes the "tremendous sense of confidentiality" that a person should have because this company operates out-of-state. The implication is that the people you may work with locally will blab your personal, confidential information to everyone they meet at the supermarket. But, they are under no obligation to keep your information private (unlike lawyers who are bound by the attorney-client privilege) and they admittedly share your information with others who may benefit from your information.

My warning to you is to not work with people outside of your state. First, lawyers can't really cross state lines so the person or company you are working with is most likely not a lawyer. Second, you can't really know what kind of operation the person or company is running. In this case, it's good to see with your own eyes to determine whether the person or company is reputable. Finally, many of these companies have been sued and have faced criminal charges for selling products the consumer do not need in the first place.

When should you seek help from an estate planning lawyer?

Even the simplest of plans can benefit from the guidance of an experienced estate planning attorney, but certain individuals should not forgo the personalized guidance of an attorney, including those who:

- Are separated or recently divorced

- Are in a second, third or later marriage

- Are not married, but in a domestic partnership

- Are in a same sex marriage or partnership

- Have step children

- Have adopted children

- Have a family member who requires specialized medical care

- Want to gift biological children different amounts

- Have foreign heirs

- Own real property

- Own foreign real estate or property in other states

- Own a business

- Have significant IRA or 401(k) assets

- Have a net worth of over $1 million

- Owe on estate taxes

- Want to avoid probate through the use of trusts

- Want to donate part of your estate to charity

- Want to use irrevocable trusts to protect assets

Even if you do choose to use an online will drafting site or software, everyone can benefit from having an experienced estate planning and probate lawyer review their will and overall estate plan.

Whether you already have an estate plan, are working on developing one, or just now considering getting started, it's best to set up a free consultation with an experienced Georgia estate planning and probate lawyer and get their advice on how best to meet your goals.

After your free consultation, an estate planning lawyer will be able to write up a price quote on several options that would work best for you.

How to Select an Estate Planning Lawyer

Selecting your Georgia Estate Planning and Probate Lawyer could be the single most important decision you make. The right lawyer can mean the difference between a successful distribution of your estate and significant loss of your estate to probate lawyer fees, the Georgia Department of Revenue and the IRS.

Because of the complex Georgia estate planning and probate process, making certain that your wishes are fulfilled successfully requires a Georgia estate planning and probate lawyer with the specialized expertise and resources required to create a thorough, legally valid and maximized estate plan.

Here are a few factors to consider in hiring an experienced Georgia estate planning attorney:

Tailor-Made Estate Plans

You, your family, and your legacy are unique. Whether you are planning for long-term care, providing for a special needs child, or preserving your children's inheritance, we can craft the individualized estate planning strategy you need.

Farrell Law Firm estate planning programs never use a cookie-cutter approach for resolving matters of probate or Medicare planning, nor do we resort to using a rote formula to write up estate planning documents. We tailor each estate plan to our client's specific goals, whether that includes ensuring you can afford a nursing home, take care of a special needs child, protect your child's inheritance after a divorce, and more.

Disability Documents for Every Estate Plan

Establishing a financial power of attorney and an advance directive for healthcare is crucial for everybody—no exceptions. The Farrell Law Firm ensures that our clients get these most important estate planning documents.

Personalized Assistance

At The Farrell Law Firm, we encourage ongoing and frequent communication. We are available to answer your questions at your convenience and work to promptly address any changes to your estate plan or any changes in the law that may affect your estate plan. Our clients are always welcome to contact us with their concerns and know they will have their questions answered right away. We are also willing to schedule phone or office meetings for more lengthy discussions.

Creative Financing

We understand that your estate and your family's future is important to you. This is why The Farrell Law Firm offers flexible financing options that helps make our customized and comprehensive estate planning affordable.

Industry Recognition

Our Farrell Law Firm estate planning and probate attorney and staff include renown professionals who are recognized as leaders in the industry. Farrell Law Firm estate planning attorney John P. Farrell is an active member of both the Georgia Bar Association and Cobb Bar Association. Licensed in both Georgia and Tennessee, John Farrell serves as a frequent lecturer on estate planning.

At The Farrell Law Firm, our mission is to ensure that you have the knowledge, resources, and legal documentation needed to preserve and pass down your legacy. We will work one on one with you to tailor an estate planning strategy to you and your unique needs and in the future when you need to make updates or modifications. We are dedicated to helping you find peace of mind and take care of your loved ones.

APPENDIX

GEORGIA SAMPLE ("STATUTORY") POWER OF ATTORNEY FORM

State of Georgia

County of _____

Georgia Statutory Form Power of Attorney
Important Information

This power of attorney authorizes another person (your agent) to make decisions concerning your property for you (the principal). Your agent will be able to make decisions and act with respect to your property (including your money) whether or not you are able to act for yourself. The meaning of authority over subjects listed on this form is explained in O.C.G.A. Chapter 6B of Title 10.

This power of attorney does not authorize the agent to make health-care decisions for you.

You should select someone you trust to serve as your agent. Unless you specify otherwise, generally the agent's authority will continue until you die or revoke the power of attorney or the agent resigns or is unable to act for you. If you revoke the power of attorney, you must communicate your revocation by notice to the agent in writing by certified mail and file such notice with the clerk of superior court in your county of domicile.

Your agent is not entitled to any compensation unless you state otherwise in the Special Instructions. Your agent shall be entitled to reimbursement of reasonable expenses incurred in performing the acts required by you in your power of attorney.

This form provides for designation of one agent. If you wish to name more than one agent you may name a successor agent or name a coagent in the Special Instructions. Coagents will not be required to act together unless you include that requirement in the Special Instructions.

If your agent is unable or unwilling to act for you, your power of attorney will end unless you have named a successor agent. You may also name a second successor agent.

This power of attorney shall be durable unless you state otherwise in the Special Instructions.

This power of attorney becomes effective immediately unless you state otherwise in the Special Instructions.

If you have questions about the power of attorney or the authority you are granting to your agent, you should seek legal advice before signing this form.

DESIGNATION OF AGENT

I, _____ (Name of Principal), name the following person as my agent:

Name of agent:

Agent's address:

Agent's telephone number:

Agent's e-mail address:

DESIGNATION OF SUCCESSOR AGENT(S) (OPTIONAL)

If my agent is unable or unwilling to act for me, I name as my successor agent:

Name of successor agent:

Successor agent's address:

Successor agent's telephone number:

Successor agent's e-mail address:

If my successor agent is unable or unwilling to act for me, I name as my second successor agent:

Name of second successor agent:

Second successor agent's address:

Second successor agent's telephone number:

Second successor agent's e-mail address:

GRANT OF GENERAL AUTHORITY

I grant my agent and any successor agent general authority to act for me with respect to the following subjects as defined in O.C.G.A. Chapter 6B of Title 10.

(INITIAL each subject you want to include in the agent's general authority. If you wish to grant general authority over all of the subjects you may initial "All Preceding Subjects" instead of initialing each subject.)

(___) Real property
(___) Tangible personal property
(___) Stocks and bonds
(___) Commodities and options
(___) Banks and other financial institutions
(___) Operation of entity or business
(___) Insurance and annuities

(___) Estates, trusts, and other beneficial interests

(___) Claims and litigation

(___) Personal and family maintenance

(___) Benefits from governmental programs or civil or military service

(___) Retirement plans

(___) Taxes

(___) All preceding subjects

GRANT OF SPECIFIC AUTHORITY (OPTIONAL)

My agent SHALL NOT do any of the following specific acts for me UNLESS I have INITIALED the specific authority listed below:

(CAUTION: Granting any of the following will give your agent the authority to take actions that could significantly reduce your property or change how your property is distributed at your death. INITIAL ONLY the specific authority you WANT to give your agent. You should give your agent specific instructions in the Special Instructions when you authorize your agent to make gifts.)

(___) Create, amend, revoke, or terminate an inter vivos trust

(___) Make a gift, subject to the limitations of O.C.G.A. § 10-6B-56 and any Special Instructions in this power of attorney

(___) Create or change rights of survivorship

(___) Create or change a beneficiary designation

(___) Authorize another person to exercise the authority granted under this power of attorney

(___) Waive the principal's right to be a beneficiary of a joint and survivor annuity, including a survivor benefit under a retirement plan

(___) Access the content of electronic communications

(___) Exercise fiduciary powers that the principal has authority to delegate

(___) Disclaim or refuse an interest in property, including a power of appointment

LIMITATIONS ON AGENT'S AUTHORITY

An agent that is not my ancestor, spouse or descendant SHALL NOT use my property to benefit the agent or a person to whom the agent owes an obligation of support unless I have included that authority in the Special Instructions.

SPECIAL INSTRUCTIONS (OPTIONAL)

You may give special instructions on the following lines (you may add lines or place your special instructions in a separate document and attach it to the power of attorney):

EFFECTIVE DATE

This power of attorney is effective immediately unless I have stated otherwise in the Special Instructions.

NOMINATION OF CONSERVATOR (OPTIONAL)

If it becomes necessary for a court to appoint a conservator of my estate, I nominate the following person(s) for appointment:

Name of nominee for conservator of my estate:

Nominee's address:

Nominee's telephone number:

Nominee's e-mail address:

RELIANCE ON THIS POWER OF ATTORNEY

Any person, including my agent, may rely upon the validity of this power of attorney or a copy of it unless that person as actual knowledge it has terminated or is invalid.

SIGNATURE AND ACKNOWLEDGMENTS

_____

_____
_____, Principal

Date

Your address
Your telephone
Your e-mail address

This document was signed in my presence on the _____, by _____.

Witness's Signature

Witness's name printed

_____

_____

Witness's address
Witness's telephone number
Witness's email address

State of Georgia

County of _____

This document was signed in my presence on the _____, by _____.

[Seal, if any]

Signature of Notary

My   commission   expires:

_____

This document prepared by: _____

IMPORTANT INFORMATION FOR AGENT
Agent's Duties

When you accept the authority granted under this power of attorney, a special legal relationship is created between you and the principal. This relationship imposes upon you legal duties that continue until you resign or the power of attorney is terminated or revoked.

You must:

(1)   Do what you know the principal reasonably expects you to do with the principal's property or, if you do not know the principal's expectations, act in the principal's best interest;

(2)   Act in good faith;

(3)   Do nothing beyond the authority granted in this power of attorney; and

(4)   Disclose your identity as an agent whenever you act for the principal by writing or printing the name of the principal and signing your own name as "agent" in the following manner:

_____ by _____ as Agent
(Principal's name)   (Your Signature)

Unless the Special Instructions in this power of attorney state otherwise, you must also:

(1)   Act loyally for the principal's benefit;

(2)   Avoid conflicts that would impair your ability to act in the principal's best interest;

(3)   Act with care, competence, and diligence;

(4)   Keep a record of all receipts, disbursements, and transactions made on behalf of the principal;

(5)   Cooperate with any person that has authority to make health-care decisions for the principal to do what you know the principal reasonably expects or, if you do not know the

principal's expectations, to act in the principal's best interest; and

(6)   Attempt to preserve the principal's estate plan if you know the plan and preserving the plan is consistent with the principal's best interest.

Termination of Agent's Authority

You must stop acting on behalf of the principal if you learn of any event that terminates this power of attorney or your authority under this power of attorney. Events that terminate a power of attorney or your authority to act under a power of attorney include:

(1)   Death of the principal;

(2)   The principal's revocation of your authority or the power of attorney so long as the revocation of the power of attorney is communicated to you in writing by certified mail and provided that such notice is filed with the clerk of superior court in the county of domicile of the principal;

(3)   The occurrence of a termination event stated in the power of attorney;

(4)   The purpose of the power of attorney is fully accomplished; or

(5)   If you are married to the principal, a legal action is filed with a court to end your marriage, or for your legal separation, unless the Special Instructions in this power of attorney state that such an action will not terminate your authority.

Liability of Agent

The meaning of the authority granted to you is defined in O.C.G.A. Chapter 6B of Title 10. If you violate O.C.G.A. Chapter 6B of Title 10, or act outside the authority granted, you may be liable for any damages caused by your violation.

If there is anything about this document or your duties that you do not understand, you should seek legal advice.

GEORGIA ADVANCE DIRECTIVE FOR HEALTH CARE FORM

GEORGIA ADVANCE DIRECTIVE FOR HEALTH CARE

By: _____ Date of Birth: _____

This advance directive for health care has four parts:

PART ONE

HEALTH CARE AGENT. *This part allows you to choose someone to make health care decisions for you when you cannot (or do not want to) make health care decisions for yourself. The person you choose is called a health care agent. You may also have your health care agent make decisions for you after your death with respect to an autopsy, organ donation, body donation, and final disposition of your body. You should talk to your health care agent about this important role.*

PART TWO

TREATMENT PREFERENCES. *This part allows you to state your treatment preferences if you have a terminal condition or if you are in a state of permanent unconsciousness. PART TWO will become effective only if you are unable to communicate your treatment preferences. Reasonable and appropriate efforts will be made to communicate with you about your treatment preferences before PART TWO becomes effective. You should talk to your family and others close to you about your treatment preferences.*

PART THREE

GUARDIANSHIP. *This part allows you to nominate a person to be your guardian should one ever be needed.*

PART FOUR

EFFECTIVENESS AND SIGNATURES. *This part requires your signature and the signatures of two witnesses. You must complete PART FOUR if you have filled out any other part of this form.*

You may fill out any or all of the first three parts listed above. You must fill out PART FOUR of this form in order for this form to be effective.

You should give a copy of this completed form to people who might need it, such as your health care agent, your family, and your physician. Keep a copy of this completed form at home in a place where it can easily be found if it is needed. Review this completed form periodically to make sure it still reflects your preferences. If your preferences change, complete a new advance directive for health care. Using this form of advance directive for health care is completely optional. Other forms of advance directives for health care may be used in Georgia.

You may revoke this completed form at any time. This completed form will replace any advance directive for health care, durable power of attorney for health care, health care proxy, or living will that you have completed before completing this form.

PART ONE

HEALTH CARE AGENT

[PART ONE will be effective even if PART TWO is not completed. A physician or health care provider who is directly involved in your health care may not serve as your health care agent. If you are married, a future divorce or annulment of your marriage will revoke the selection of your current spouse as your health care agent. If you are not married, a future marriage will revoke the selection of your health care agent unless the person you selected as your health care agent is your new spouse.]

(1) HEALTH CARE AGENT

I select the following person as my health care agent to make health care decisions for me:

Name:

Address:

Telephone Numbers:

(Home, Work, and Mobile)

(2) BACK-UP HEALTH CARE AGENT

[This section is optional. PART ONE will be effective even if this section is left blank.]

If my health care agent cannot be contacted in a reasonable time period and cannot be located with reasonable efforts or for any reason my health care agent is unavailable or unable or unwilling to act as my health care agent, then I select the following, each to act successively in the order named, as my back-up health care agent(s):

Name:

Address:

Telephone Numbers:

(Home, Work, and Mobile)

Name:

Address:

Telephone Numbers:

(Home, Work, and Mobile)

(3) GENERAL POWERS OF HEALTH CARE AGENT

My health care agent will make health care decisions for me when I am unable to communicate my health care decisions or I choose to have my health care agent communicate my health care decisions. My health care agent will have the same authority to make any health care decision that I could make. My health care agent's authority includes, for example, the power to:

> Admit me to or discharge me from any hospital, skilled nursing facility, hospice, or other health care facility or service;
>
> Request, consent to, withhold, or withdraw any type of health care; and
>
> Contract for any health care facility or service for me, and to obligate me to pay for these services (and my health care agent will not be financially liable for any services or care contracted for me or on my behalf).

My health care agent will be my personal representative for all purposes of federal or state law related to privacy of medical records (including the Health Insurance Portability and Accountability Act of

1996) and will have the same access to my medical records that I have and can disclose the contents of my medical records to others for my ongoing health care.

My health care agent may accompany me in an ambulance or air ambulance if in the opinion of the ambulance personnel protocol permits a passenger and my health care agent may visit or consult with me in person while I am in a hospital, skilled nursing facility, hospice, or other health care facility or service if its protocol permits visitation. My health care agent may present a copy of this advance directive for health care in lieu of the original and the copy will have the same meaning and effect as the original.

I understand that under Georgia law:

My health care agent may refuse to act as my health care agent; A court can take away the powers of my health care agent if it finds that my health care agent is not acting properly; and

My health care agent does not have the power to make health care decisions for me regarding psychosurgery, sterilization, or treatment or involuntary hospitalization for mental or emotional illness, mental retardation, or addictive disease.

(4) GUIDANCE FOR HEALTH CARE AGENT

When making health care decisions for me, my health care agent should think about what action would be consistent with past conversations we have had, my treatment preferences as expressed in PART TWO (if I have filled out PART TWO), my religious and other beliefs and values, and how I have handled medical and other important issues in the past. If what I would decide is still unclear, then my health care agent should make decisions for me that my health care agent believes are in my best interest, considering the benefits, burdens, and risks of my current circumstances and treatment options.

(5) POWERS OF HEALTH CARE AGENT AFTER DEATH
(A) AUTOPSY

My health care agent will have the power to authorize an autopsy of my body unless I have limited my health care agent's power by initialing below.

_____ (Initials) My health care agent will not have the power to authorize an autopsy of my body (unless an autopsy is required by law).

(B) ORGAN DONATION AND DONATION OF BODY

My health care agent will have the power to make a disposition of any part or all of my body for medical purposes pursuant to the Georgia Anatomical Gift Act, unless I have limited my health care agent's power by initialing below.

[Initial each statement that you want to apply.]

_____ (Initials) My health care agent will not have the power to make a disposition of my body for use in a medical study program.

_____ (Initials) My health care agent will not have the power to donate any of my organs.

(C) FINAL DISPOSITION OF BODY

My health care agent will have the power to make decisions about the final disposition of my body unless I have initialed below.

_____ (Initials) I want the following person to make decisions about the final disposition of my body:

Name:

Address:

Telephone Numbers:

(Home, Work, and Mobile)

I wish for my body to be:

_____ (Initials) Buried

OR

_____ (Initials) Cremated

PART TWO:
TREATMENT PREFERENCES

[PART TWO will be effective only if you are unable to communicate your treatment preferences after reasonable and appropriate efforts have been made to communicate with you about your treatment preferences. PART TWO will be effective even if PART ONE is not completed. If you have not selected a health care agent in PART ONE, or if your health care agent is not available, then PART TWO will

provide your physician and other health care providers with your treatment preferences. If you have selected a health care agent in PART ONE, then your health care agent will have the authority to make all health care decisions for you regarding matters covered by PART TWO. Your health care agent will be guided by your treatment preferences and other factors described in Section (4) of PART ONE.]

(6) CONDITIONS

PART TWO will be effective if I am in any of the following conditions:

[Initial each condition in which you want PART TWO to be effective.]

_____ (Initials) A terminal condition, which means I have an incurable or irreversible condition that will result in my death in a relatively short period of time.

_____ (Initials) A state of permanent unconsciousness, which means I am in an incurable or irreversible condition in which I am not aware of myself or my environment and I show no behavioral response to my environment.

My condition will be determined in writing after personal examination by my attending physician and a second physician in accordance with currently accepted medical standards.

(7) TREATMENT PREFERENCES

[State your treatment preference by initialing (A), (B), or (C). If you choose (C), state your additional treatment preferences by initialing one or more of the statements following (C). You may provide additional instructions about your treatment preferences in the next section. You will be provided with comfort care, including pain relief, but you may also want to state your specific preferences regarding pain relief in the next section.]

If I am in any condition that I initialed in Section (6) above and I can no longer communicate my treatment preferences after reasonable and appropriate efforts have been made to communicate with me about my treatment preferences, then:

(A) _____ (Initials) Try to extend my life for as long as possible, using all medications, machines, or other medical procedures that in reasonable medical judgment could keep me alive. If I am unable to take

nutrition or fluids by mouth, then I want to receive nutrition or fluids by tube or other medical means.
OR
(B) _____ (Initials) Allow my natural death to occur. I do not want any medications, machines, or other medical procedures that in reasonable medical judgment could keep me alive but cannot cure me. I do not want to receive nutrition or fluids by tube or other medical means except as needed to provide pain medication.
OR
(C) _____ (Initials) I do not want any medications, machines, or other medical procedures that in reasonable medical judgment could keep me alive but cannot cure me, except as follows:
[Initial each statement that you want to apply to option (C).]

_____ (Initials) If I am unable to take nutrition by mouth, I want to receive nutrition by tube or other medical means.

_____ (Initials) If I am unable to take fluids by mouth, I want to receive fluids by tube or other medical means.

_____ (Initials) If I need assistance to breathe, I want to have a ventilator used.

_____ (Initials) If my heart or pulse has stopped, I want to have cardiopulmonary resuscitation (CPR) used.

(8) ADDITIONAL STATEMENTS

*[**This section is optional.** PART TWO will be effective even if this section is left blank. This section allows you to state additional treatment preferences, to provide additional guidance to your health care agent (if you have selected a health care agent in PART ONE), or to provide information about your personal and religious values about your medical treatment. For example, you may want to state your treatment preferences regarding medications to fight infection, surgery, amputation, blood transfusion, or kidney dialysis.*

Understanding that you cannot foresee everything that could happen to you after you can no longer communicate your treatment preferences, you may want to provide guidance to your health care agent (if you have selected a health care agent in PART ONE) about following your treatment preferences. You may want to state your specific preferences regarding pain relief.]

(9) IN CASE OF PREGNANCY

[PART TWO will be effective even if this section is left blank.]
I understand that under Georgia law, PART TWO generally will have no force and effect if I am pregnant unless the fetus is not viable and I indicate by initialing below that I want PART TWO to be carried out.

_____ (Initials) I want PART TWO to be carried out if my fetus is not viable.

PART THREE:
GUARDIANSHIP
(10) GUARDIANSHIP

*[**PART THREE is optional.** This advance directive for health care will be effective even if PART THREE is left blank. If you wish to nominate a person to be your guardian in the event a court decides that a guardian should be appointed, complete PART THREE. A court will appoint a guardian for you if the court finds that you are not able to make significant responsible decisions for yourself regarding your personal support, safety, or welfare. A court will appoint the person nominated by you if the court finds that the appointment will serve your best interest and welfare. If you have selected a health care agent in PART ONE, you may (but are not required to) nominate the same person to be your guardian. If your health care agent and guardian are not the same person, your health care agent will have priority over your guardian in making your health care decisions, unless a court determines otherwise.]*

[State your preference by initialing (A) or (B). Choose (A) only if you have also completed PART ONE.]

    (A) _____ (Initials) I nominate the person serving as my health care agent under PART ONE to serve as my guardian.
    OR

(B) _____ (Initials) I nominate the following person to serve as my guardian:

Name:

Address:

Telephone Numbers:

(Home, Work, and Mobile)

PART FOUR:
EFFECTIVENESS AND SIGNATURES

This advance directive for health care will become effective only if I am unable or choose not to make or communicate my own health care decisions.

This form revokes any advance directive for health care, durable power of attorney for health care, health care proxy, or living will that I have completed before this date.

Unless I have initialed below and have provided alternative future dates or events, this advance directive for health care will become effective at the time I sign it and will remain effective until my death (and after my death to the extent authorized in Section (5) of PART ONE).

_____ (Initials) This advance directive for health care will become effective on or upon _____ and will terminate on or upon _____.

[You must sign and date or acknowledge signing and dating this form in the presence of two witnesses.

Both witnesses must be of sound mind and must be at least 18 years of age, but the witnesses do not have to be together or present with you when you sign this form.

A witness:

> *Cannot be a person who was selected to be your health care agent or back-up health care agent in PART ONE;*
> *Cannot be a person who will knowingly inherit anything from you or otherwise knowingly gain a financial benefit from your death; or*
> *Cannot be a person who is directly involved in your health care.*

Only one of the witnesses may be an employee, agent, or medical staff member of the hospital, skilled nursing facility, hospice, or other health care facility in which you are receiving health care (but this witness cannot be directly involved in your health care).]

By signing below, I state that I am emotionally and mentally capable of making this advance directive for health care and that I understand its purpose and effect.

(Signature of Declarant)

(Date)

The declarant signed this form in my presence or acknowledged signing this form to me. Based upon my personal observation, the declarant appeared to be emotionally and mentally capable of making this advance directive for health care and signed this form willingly and voluntarily.

(Signature of First Witness)

(Date)

Print Name:

Address:

(Signature of Second Witness)

(Date)

Print Name:

Address:

[This form does not need to be notarized.]

GLOSSARY OF COMMON TERMS

Here is a list of some of the terms used in this guide and commonly in estate planning. This list is not exhaustive. If you have any questions about what a term means, contact an experienced estate planning attorney.

Codicil
Written amendment or change to an existing Last Will and Testament.

Deed
Written document which transfers ownership of property from one person or company to another person or company.

Disclaimer
Refusal to accept an inheritance so it may pass to the next person in line.

Disinherit
Purposefully choosing to keep someone from inheriting assets.

Estate Tax
Federal or state tax placed on the value of one's assets following their death. Also called the "death tax."

Executor/Personal Representative
Person named in a Will who will handle the administrative process of probating a Will. Where a Trustee handles the administration of a

Trust, an Executor (or Personal Representative depending on the state) handles the administration of a Will.

Funding

Act of transferring assets to your Trust. Typically done during the trust maker's lifetime in order to make the trust work efficiently. Many people confuse this term with the idea that money/currency is added to the trust, but this also includes things like real estate, membership interests in limited liability corporations, etc. Otherwise, the asset may have to go through the probate process. Funding the trust is probably the most important part of creating a trust.

Heir

Person who is entitled by law to receive part of an estate.

Holographic Will

Will written by hand.

Inheritance Tax

State tax placed on the assets a person receives by inheritance.

Intestate/Intestacy

When someone passes away without a Will to dispose of their property. If you don't describe how you want your property to pass and to whom you want the property to go through a Will or Trust, then the state will decide how and to whom your property will go.

Joint Tenancy with Rights of Survivorship

Type of ownership where two (or more) owners jointly own the same property. When one owner dies, his or her share passes to the other owners of the property.

Last Will and Testament

Written document with instructions on how the assets of a deceased person's assets will be distributed. This document and its provisions can only be enforced by the Probate Court.

Living Will
Written document stating your desires and wishes regarding the withholding or withdrawing of life support systems. Not to be confused with a Last Will and Testament.

Probate
Legal process of validating a will, paying debts of the decedent, and distributing the remaining assets to the heirs.

Pour-Over Will
While also being a Last Will and Testament, it is not designed to dispose of a person's entire estate. Used in conjunction with a person's trust to catch things that are not caught, or "pour-over," by the trust. Typically, these are much smaller than a Last Will and Testament that is used to dispose of someone's entire estate.

Tenants-in-Common
Type of ownership where two (or more) owners jointly own the same property. When one owner dies, his or her share passes to his or her heirs.

Testate
When someone passes with a Last Will and Testament. The opposite of "intestate."

Unfunded
Trust which hasn't had any assets transferred into it (considered a dirty word in the estate planning world).

TESTIMONIALS

What Others Say About Mr. Farrell and his Staff

"Mr. Farrell was very helpful and professional in completing our will and estate. He has a wonderful sense of humor and is very personable – he made us comfortable to discuss and make decisions on the end of life matters. He helped us on things we never would have thought about. He is very thorough and available for any questions we may have. Knowing he will be there for us now until the end is very comforting and we now have peace of mind! Thank you, John Farrell!"

– Lori M., Powder Springs, Georgia

"I found John's services to be very easy, straightforward and professional. Information was provided in simple and clear definitions. The supporting staff was very helpful. Overall, a positive experience with warm, caring people."

- Heather P., Marietta, Georgia

"Personable, professional, proficient!!"

- Diana D., Kennesaw, Georgia

"John is simply in a word "excellent." He is both professional and thoughtful – taking time to understand his clients' goals and hopes so that he can best reflect them in their estate plans. We highly recommend him."

– Robert and Ingrid C., Atlanta, Georgia

"John Farrell was wonderful to work with. He was very thorough and made the estate planning process very simple and easy for us to complete. He was always prompt at responding to our questions. We highly recommend The Farrell Law Firm."

- Paul and Elizabeth R., Marietta, Georgia

"John was very thorough, courteous, and extremely helpful in guiding us to make decisions concerning estate planning. He patiently answered all our questions and clarified any concerns we had. We would highly recommend Farrell Law Firm and their services!"

- Kent and Lyn D., Powder Springs, Georgia

"Thank you, John Farrell, for handling our trust planning. John was very courteous and thorough in guiding us through the process. All of our questions and concerns were addressed. We received our estate planning portfolio in a timely manner and we would highly recommend Farrell Law services to anyone."

- Elaine H., Marietta, Georgia

"We chose John because of being an Estate Planning attorney. We found him to be very organized and professional. He is easy to talk to and we feel comfortable with asking him anything. Our first meeting with him gave us a lot to think about, so when we returned to finalize our Will, we felt confident in our own decisions. We received a draft in the mail prior to our final meeting, which was very helpful to prepare for the signing. The Estate Planning Portfolio organized everything for us and our loved ones. John made this an easy process for us."

- Chip and Rosemary S., Woodstock, Georgia

"Mr. Farrell was very prompt; courteous. He covered all bases with no questions needed to be asked and was willing to walk through everything we needed."

- Ron T., Marietta, Georgia

"John Farrell is magnificent! I met with him and was very impressed with the information regarding Estate Planning and the cost of preparation. John Farrell took over all of my concerns regarding the estate and answered all of my questions. I am thrilled with the Estate Plan and all of the positive results that are now established for my family. Thank You!"

- Lynne R., Calhoun, Georgia

"Thanks for helping us get our wills updated and in order. You were very professional and yet very good at explaining in layman's terms. We never felt rushed or pushed into any decisions and we appreciated your willingness to answer all our questions. We felt like we were dealing with someone we could trust. We wish you well in your law practice, and personal life."

- Jere and Gwen A., Acworth, Georgia

"We found John to be very friendly, made our experience personable, very informative and understanding our need for fast service and delivered a well-done product."

- Richard P., Kennesaw, Georgia

"Mr. Farrell was very conscientious and professional. He did not hurry us with our many questions about planning and settling estates."

- Sherry K., Marietta, Georgia

"Our search for an attorney to handle our Wills, Advance Directives, and Estate Trust led us to Farrell Law. We found the knowledge and professional expertise we were looking for. The group meeting we attended was very informative, and our personal meetings have been well-organized and thorough. We have been able to place our full confidence in Mr. Farrell, and the location in Marietta is perfect for us. We are pleased that we chose John Farrell to prepare our legal documents and serve as our attorney."

- David and Diane W., Marietta, Georgia

OFFICE INFORMATION

Newsletter Subscription

If you are reading this book, there's a fair chance that you also receive our free monthly e-newsletter. In this e-newsletter, we share articles about estate planning, updates to changes in Georgia law related to estate planning, office information, testimonials, and more !!

Subscribing is easy. Simply reach out to us and we'll add your name to our free monthly e-newsletter.

Call: (678) 809-4922
E-mail: John@TheFarrellLawFirm.com

Mail:
The Farrell Law Firm, P.C.
316 Alexander St., SE, Ste. 4
Marietta, Georgia 30060

Free Consultation

If you would like to schedule a free consultation with an attorney at the Farrell Law Firm, please contact us at our office above.

Made in the USA
Columbia, SC
31 January 2024

30804985R00095